ANALYSIS OF BANK FINANCIAL STATEMENTS

Oliver G. Wood, Jr.
and
Robert J. Porter
University of South Carolina

VNR VAN NOSTRAND REINHOLD COMPANY
NEW YORK   CINCINNATI   ATLANTA   DALLAS   SAN FRANCISCO
LONDON   TORONTO   MELBORNE

For
Brian and Patricia
and
Ella Mae

Van Nostrand Reinhold Company Regional Offices:
New York Cincinnati Atlanta Dallas San Francisco

Van Nostrand Reinhold Company International Offices:
London Toronto Melbourne

Copyright © 1979 by Litton Educational Publishing, Inc.

Library of Congress Catalog Card Number: 78-24312
ISBN: 0-442-29537-5

Manufactured in the United States of America

Published by Van Nostrand Reinhold Company
135 West 50th Street, New York, N.Y. 10020

Published simultaneously in Canada by Van Nostrand Reinhold Ltd.

15 14 13 12 11 10 9 8 7 6 5 4 3 2 1

Library of Congress Cataloging in Publication Data

Wood, Oliver G. Jr. 1937-
    Analysis of bank financial statements.

    Includes bibliographical references and index.
    1. Banks and banking—Accounting. I. Porter,
Robert J., joint author. II. Title.
HG1708.W58   657'.833   78-24312
ISBN 0-442-29537-5

Preface

The failures of U.S. National Bank of San Diego in 1973 and Franklin National Bank in 1974 shocked the banking industry. The general feeling was "if these billion-dollar banks could fail, then every bank is a potential failure." Many bankers realized for the first time that federal funds sold to another bank may not be a riskless asset. This possibility underscored the need for banks to have up-to-date information on the financial condition of every bank with whom they have a relationship.

Bank regulatory authorities also stepped up efforts to improve their analysis of bank financial condition. Research was concentrated on finding those financial variables from regularly reported financial statements and other data that would provide an "early warning system" of deteriorating financial condition. A notable example of such a system is the National Bank Surveillance System (NBSS) developed by the office of the Comptroller of the Currency to assist the Comptroller in the early detection of problem banks and bank management to initiate early corrective action.

While the primary thrust of this book is toward financial analysis of the individual bank's performance, the ratios and techniques developed also are applied to aggregate data for the banking system. Trends are shown in liquidity, capital, and profitability ratios, by bank size classes. This will permit the comparative evaluation of individual bank performance with peer group averages.

The aim of *Analysis of Bank Financial Statements* is to provide a concise explanation of the basic ratios and techniques used in the analysis of bank financial statements. Although intended primarily for bank officers, this book also should be useful to investors, security analysts, and corporate cash managers; as a supplementary text in college banking and finance courses; and in the various banking schools. Chapter 1 contains a description of the nature and functions of each bank asset, liability, and capital account. Chapter 2 is on bank liquidity analysis. Basic bank liquidity concepts are discussed, and a relatively simple system for liquidity analysis by management is explained. In addition, the major liquidity ratios are explained and evaluated for use by those with access only to published financial statements.

Chapter 3 deals with the nature and functions of bank capital and the measurement of capital adequacy by both management and "outsiders." Chapter 4 contains a description of each item on the bank income statement. Chapter 5 has a discussion of the traditional profitability ratios. Chapter 6, "Profit Sensitivity Analysis," contains an explanation of how to impute changes in income and expenses to changes in interest rates and/or levels of earning assets and interest-costing liabilities. These relatively new techniques are used by every major bank in the country. In addition, a chart is developed that explains the relationship among the principal determinants of a bank's return on equity capital. Finally, the key early warning signals of changes in bank financial condition are set forth in Chapter 7.

The authors wish to thank William C. Barksdale, Vice-President and Administrator of Commercial Loans at the South Carolina National Bank, for helpful comments and suggestions on the manuscript. Also, we are appreciative of the very excellent assistance provided by Gene Falken and Michelle Herman at Van Nostrand Reinhold.

Oliver G. Wood, Jr.
Robert J. Porter

LIST OF TABLES

LIST OF FIGURES

Contents

1
Bank Assets, Liabilities, and Capital

We will begin our study of bank financial analysis with the *statement of condition* or balance sheet. This statement reflects the bank's assets, liabilities, and capital on one specific date; for example, December 31. *Bank assets* are "things owned," such as cash in vault, loans, securities, and buildings. *Bank liabilities* are non-owner claims on the bank's assets, examples of which are demand deposits, savings deposits, bills payable, and other expenses. *Bank equity capital* represents the book value of shareholder claims on the bank's assets. This investment is measured by the sum of the common stock, surplus, and undivided profits accounts. All assets are matched by the sum of the non-owner and shareholder claims. Thus, the basic bank balance sheet equation is assets equal liabilities plus equity capital.

BANK ASSETS

Bank assets represent *uses* of bank funds. In the first part of this chapter, we will examine each of the major types of bank assets and explain why banks hold assets in these forms. Figure 1-1 contains the "Report of Condition" as required by the Comptroller of the Currency for national banks. This format is very similar to that required by the Federal Deposit Insurance Corportation (FDIC) for state, non-member, insured banks and by the Federal Reserve for state, member banks.

NAME OF BANK: _____ CHARTER NUMBER: _____

BALANCE SHEET at the close of business on _____

Statement of Resources and Liabilities

		Sch.	Item	Col.				Thousands of dollars		
					month	day	year	THOUSANDS	Hnds.	Cts.
ASSETS	1. Cash and due from banks	C	7					XXX	XX	1
	2. U.S. Treasury securities	B	1	E				XXX	XX	2
	3. Obligations of other U.S. Gov't. agencies and corps.	B	2	E				XXX	XX	3
	4. Obligations of States and political subdivisions	B	3	E				XXX	XX	4
	5. Other bonds, notes, and debentures	B	4	E				XXX	XX	5
	6. Federal Reserve stock and corporate stock							XXX	XX	6
	7. Trading account securities							XXX	XX	7
	8. Federal funds sold and securities purchased under agreements to resell	D	4					XXX	XX	8
	9. a. Loans, Total (excluding unearned income)	A	10		XXX	XX				9a
	b. Less: Reserve for possible loan losses				XXX	XX				b
	c. Loans, Net							XXX	XX	c
	10. Direct lease financing							XXX	XX	10
	11. Bank premises, furniture and fixtures, and other assets representing bank premises							XXX	XX	11
	12. Real estate owned other than bank premises							XXX	XX	12
	13. Investments in unconsolidated subsidiaries and associated companies							XXX	XX	13
	14. Customers' liability to this bank on acceptances outstanding							XXX	XX	14
	15. Other assets	G	7					XXX	XX	15
	16. TOTAL ASSETS (sum of Items 1 thru 15)	F						XXX	XX	16
LIABILITIES	17. Demand deposits of individuals, prtnshps., and corps.	F	1f	A				XXX	XX	17
	18. Time and savings deposits of individuals, prtnshps., and corps.	F	1f	B+C				XXX	XX	18
	19. Deposits of United States Government	F	2	A+B+C				XXX	XX	19
	20. Deposits of States and political subdivisions	F	3	A+B+C				XXX	XX	20
	21. Deposits of foreign govts. and official institutions	F	4	A+B+C				XXX	XX	21
	22. Deposits of commercial banks	F	5+6	A+B+C				XXX	XX	22
	23. Certified and officers' checks	F	7	A				XXX	XX	23
	24. TOTAL DEPOSITS (sum of Items 17 thru 23)							XXX	XX	24
	a. Total demand deposits	F	8	A	XXX	XX				a
	b. Total time and savings deposits	F	8	B+C	XXX	XX				b
	25. Federal funds purchased and securities sold under agreements to repurchase	E	4					XXX	XX	25
	26. Liabilities for borrowed money							XXX	XX	26
	27. Mortgage indebtedness and liability for capitalized leases							XXX	XX	27
	28. Acceptances executed by or for account of this bank and outstanding							XXX	XX	28
	29. Other liabilities	H	9					XXX	XX	29
	30. TOTAL LIABILITIES (sum of Items 24 thru 29 excluding Items 24a & b)							XXX	XX	30
	31. Subordinated notes and debentures							XXX	XX	31
EQUITY CAPITAL	32. Preferred stock No. shares outstanding _____ (par value)							XXX	XX	32
	33. Common stock a. No. shares authorized _____									
	b. No. shares outstanding _____ (par value)							XXX	XX	33
	34. Surplus							XXX	XX	34
	35. Undivided profits							XXX	XX	35
	36. Reserve for contingencies and other capital reserves							XXX	XX	36
	37. TOTAL EQUITY CAPITAL (sum of Items 32 thru 36)							XXX	XX	37
	38. TOTAL LIABILITIES AND EQUITY CAPITAL (sum of Items 30, 31, and 37)							XXX	XX	38
MEMORANDA	1. Average for 30 calendar days ending with report date:									
	a. Cash and due from banks (corresponds to Item 1 above)							XXX	XX	1a
	b. Fed. funds sold and securities purchased under agreements to resell (corresponds to Item 8 above)							XXX	XX	b
	c. Total loans (corresponds to subitem 9a above)							XXX	XX	c
	d. Time deposits of $100,000 or more (corresponds to memoranda subitems 3 plus 4 below)							XXX	XX	d
	e. Total deposits (corresponds to Item 24 above)							XXX	XX	e
	f. Fed. funds purchased and securities sold under agreements to repurchase (corr. to Item 25 above)							XXX	XX	f
	g. Liabilities for borrowed money (corresponds to Item 26 above)							XXX	XX	g
	h. TOTAL ASSETS (corresponds to Item 16 above)							XXX	XX	h
	2. Standby letters of credit (outstanding as of report date)							XXX	XX	2
	3. Time certificates of deposit in denominations of $100,000 or more (outstanding as of report date)							XXX	XX	3
	4. Other time deposits in amounts of $100,000 or more (outstanding as of report date)							XXX	XX	4

Form CC-8022-06

Figure 1-1. Bank Statement of Condition (Sample).

Cash and Due From Banks

This asset category includes all of the various bank cash assets.

- Currency and coin
- Reserves with the Federal Reserve Bank
- Deposits due from other banks
- Cash items in the process of collection

Currency and Coin. A bank's currency and coin are held in its vault. For this reason, it is usually called cash-in-vault or vault cash. A bank holds vault cash only to accommodate customers who may wish to exercise a deposit claim for currency or coin. Vault cash is a non-earning asset to the bank. It is a "cost generating" asset because the bank must pay for an expensive vault to house it; pay for insurance to cover possible losses due to theft or burglary; and pay people to count and guard it.

A commercial bank obtains currency and coin from its Federal Reserve Banks. Practically all our currency consists of Federal Reserve Notes and is issued by, and is a liability of, Federal Reserve Banks. Coins are issued by the Treasury to Federal Reserve Banks, which hold them until they are requested by commercial banks. On December 31, 1977, insured commercial banks held $13.9 billion or 1.2 percent of their assets in currency and coin.

Reserves with the Federal Reserve Bank. Banks that are members of the Federal Reserve System hold balances with their individual Federal Reserve Banks. These balances serve two primary functions. First, along with vault cash, they count as legal reserves for a member bank.[1] Second, commercial banks use their reserve balances in much the same manner as an individual uses his checking account. For credit, banks forward checks drawn on other banks throughout the country to their Federal Reserve Bank. The Federal Reserve Bank credits the sending bank in accordance with a predetermined schedule which ranges from immediate credit to two days delayed credit. Checks drawn on nearby banks are credited

[1]Legal reserves are those assets that count toward meeting a Federal Reserve or state reserve requirement.

Table 1-1   Assets and Liabilities of Insured Commercial Banks, Selected Years, 1970–1977 (Billions of Dollars).

	YEAR ENDING DECEMBER 31				
	1970	1972	1974	1976	1977
ASSETS					
Cash and due from banks	93.0	111.8	126.1	130.2	159.3
U.S. Treasury securities	58.9	64.7	51.9	96.9	95.5
Obligations of other U.S. Government agencies and corporations	12.5	21.2	31.1	34.3	35.8
Obligations of states and political subdivisions	67.4	87.4	96.8	103.5	112.4
Other bonds, notes, and debentures	2.8	5.3	6.2	5.8	5.7
Corporate stock	–	–	–	1.5	1.6
Trading account securities	5.7	5.1	8.0	7.9	6.4
Federal funds sold and securities purchased under agreements to resell	16.0	25.6	38.9	45.9	49.7
Loans, total	298.2	388.9	506.4	537.5	607.8
Loans less reserve for possible loan losses[1]	–	–	–	6.2	6.6
Loans less unearned income on loans	–	–	–	12.7	14.6
Loans, net	298.2	388.9	506.4	518.7	586.6
Direct lease financing	–	–	–	5.1	5.8
Bank premises, furniture, fixtures, and other assets representing bank premises	9.1	11.5	14.3	16.7	18.3
Real estate owned other than bank premises	.4	.4	.8	2.9	3.0
Investments in unconsolidated subsidiaries and associated companies	.7	1.1	1.7	2.3	3.0
Customers liability on acceptances outstanding	3.8	3.5	10.7	9.1	11.5
Other assets	7.9	11.1	19.7	30.4	35.4
TOTAL ASSETS	576.4	737.7	912.5	1,011.3	1,129.7
LIABILITIES AND EQUITY CAPITAL					
Demand deposits of individuals, partnerships, and corporations	181.9	221.2	236.0	255.4	286.6
Time and savings deposits of individuals, partnerships, and corporations	205.0	271.9	358.3	428.6	471.2
Deposits of U.S. Government	8.4	11.5	5.3	3.8	8.2
Deposits of states and political subdivisions	41.1	56.0	68.9	68.1	75.8
Deposits of foreign governments and official institutions	5.6	7.4	13.9	10.4	9.9
Deposits of banks in foreign countries	3.3	3.9	8.2	8.6	9.5
Deposits of commercial banks in U.S.	29.0	33.7	45.3	44.5	47.3
Certified and officers' checks	8.4	11.3	10.4	11.6	14.0
TOTAL DEPOSITS	482.5	616.9	746.4	830.9	922.6

Table 1-1 Assets and Liabilities of Insured Commercial Banks, Selected Years, 1970-1977 (Billions of Dollars). (continued)

| | YEAR ENDING DECEMBER 31 | | | | |
	1970	1972	1974	1976	1977
Demand	247.2	296.4	314.4	334.0	377.0
Savings	98.8	124.2	136.3	203.9	218.8
Time	136.5	196.3	295.7	293.0	326.8
Federal funds purchased and securities sold under agreements to repurchase	16.6	33.7	51.2	70.3	82.8
Liabilities for borrowed money	2.6	4.0	4.9	5.1	6.6
Mortgage indebtedness	.7	1.2	.7	.8	1.0
Acceptances outstanding	3.8	3.6	11.2	9.8	12.1
Other liabilities	21.3	19.1	26.1	17.0	19.8
TOTAL LIABILITIES	527.5	678.4	840.6	933.9	1,045.0
Subordinated notes and debentures	2.1	4.1	4.3	5.1	5.7
Reserves on loans and securities	6.3	6.9	8.7	—	—
EQUITY CAPITAL					
Preferred stock	.1	.1	.1	.1	.1
Common stock	11.1	12.9	14.8	16.2	17.2
Surplus	18.1	21.5	25.3	28.9	31.0
Undivided profits	10.1	13.0	18.0	25.3	29.1
Reserve for contingencies and other reserves	1.0	.8	1.0	1.8	1.8
TOTAL EQUITY CAPITAL	40.5	48.3	59.0	72.3	79.1
TOTAL LIABILITIES AND EQUITY CAPITAL	576.4	737.7	912.5	1,011.3	1,129.7

Source: FDIC, *Annual Reports* and *Federal Reserve Bulletin.*

[1]Included in "Reserves on Loans and Securities," 1970-1975.

Note: Totals may not add due to rounding.

immediately while those drawn on distant banks are credited after one or two days. A commercial bank transfers funds from its reserve balance with the Federal Reserve by writing a check on the account or by initiating a *wire transfer*, which simply involves requesting one Federal Reserve Bank to inform another over the Federal Reserve's wire facilities that it wishes to shift balances to the reserve account of another bank. On December 31, 1977, insured commercial banks held $29.3 billion or 2.6 percent of their assets in reserves with Federal Reserve Banks.

Deposits Due from Other Banks. Commercial banks hold deposits in other banks (called correspondent banks) for several reasons. First, in most states, state, non-member banks are permitted to count balances due from other banks as legal reserves. These non-member banks send checks for clearing to their correspondent banks, which, in turn, usually clear them through the Federal Reserve System. Non-member banks also may write checks on, and wire funds from, their correspondent bank accounts. Member banks also hold balances with other banks, but these funds do not count as legal reserves. Non-member and member banks alike clear checks through their correspondent bank accounts, and transfer funds from them by means of check or wire. Besides clearing checks, correspondent banks perform a variety of other services, such as loan participations, investment transactions, and assistance with international banking transactions. Thus, a second rationale for a bank to hold deposits with another bank is to compensate the bank for services performed. The appropriate size of these balances is renegotiated periodically. Virtually all correspondent balances are demand deposits. On December 31, 1977, insured commercial banks held $44.8 billion or 4.0 percent of their assets in balances due from other U.S. banks.

Cash Items in The Process of Collection. Cash items in the process of collection represent checks deposited in Federal Reserve Banks or correspondent banks for which credit has not been received. On December 31, 1977, insured commercial banks held $66.3 billion or 5.9 percent of their assets in cash items. In fact, at most banks, cash items make up the largest cash asset. The size of this asset item depends upon the volume of checks and the time it takes to clear the checks. Because this is a non-earning asset, banks strive to process and collect cash items as rapidly as possible.

U.S. Treasury Securities

The U.S. Treasury issues three primary types of marketable securities: Treasury bills, Treasury notes, and Treasury bonds. Treasury bills are the shortest term obligation, with initial maturities ranging from 91 days to 360 days. Treasury notes have initial maturities ranging from one to seven years, while Treasury bonds have initial maturities of five years or more. Treasury securities are backed by the full faith and credit of the federal government; therefore, they are considered free of the risk of default. Banks hold Treasury issues with one year or less to maturity primarily for liquidity purposes because these obligations may be converted into a cash asset very readily with little or no loss of principal. These short-term obligations can be converted to cash assets to meet deposit withdrawals, maturing liabilities and legitimate loan demands and commitments without delay. Treasury issues held with a maturity beyond one year serve two functions: (1) they provide supplementary income and (2) they provide supplementary liquidity. On December 31, 1977, insured commercial banks held $95.5 billion or 8.4 percent of their assets in Treasury obligations.

Obligations of Other U.S. Government Agencies and Corporations

There are a number of government corporations and federally sponsored agencies that issue bonds, notes, and debentures to raise funds to carry out their activities. The securities of these corporations and agencies are commonly called "agencies" and include those issued by the Export-Import Bank, Federal Intermediate Credit Banks, Federal National Mortgage Association, Government National Mortgage Association, Federal Land Banks, Federal Home Loan Banks, Banks for Cooperatives, Tennessee Valley Authority, D.C. Stadium Bonds, Federal Housing Administration debentures, and Merchant Marine Bonds. Banks hold agencies for the same reasons that they hold Treasury issues; i.e., primary liquidity, supplemental income, and secondary liquidity. It is important to note that agencies are not official obligations of the U.S. Treasury; therefore, yields tend to be slightly higher than those on Treasury issues of comparable maturity. On December 31, 1977, insured commercial banks held $35.8 billion or 3.2 percent of their assets in the form of agencies obligations.

Obligations of States and Political Subdivisions

Obligations of states and political subdivisions are commonly called "municipals." These securities include those issued by states, cities, counties, school districts, water and sewer districts, and local housing authorities.

There are two principal reasons why banks purchase municipals. First, the interest income but not the capital gain is free of federal income taxes and state income taxes if the security is held by the bank in the state of issue. Thus, if the combined federal and state income tax rate is 50 percent, a bank holding a municipal yielding 6 percent would have to earn at least 12 percent on a taxable security to achieve a comparable after-tax yield. Capital gains and losses resulting from appreciation or depreciation in market value over time are considered ordinary income and losses for tax purposes. The second primary reason that banks hold municipals is as security for deposits of states and political subdivisions. At the close of 1977, insured commercial banks held $112.4 billion or 9.9 percent of their assets in municipals.

Other Bonds, Notes, and Debentures

This asset category includes bank investment in the securities of the Asian Development Bank, foreign governmental units, Inter-American Development Bank, and the International Bank for Reconstruction and Development (World Bank). At the end of 1977, insured commercial banks held $5.7 billion or 0.5 percent of their assets in this asset class.

Federal Reserve Stock and Corporation Stock

Member banks are required to purchase stock of the Federal Reserve Bank equal to 3 percent of the common stock and surplus of the member bank. Banks receive a 6 percent tax-free dividend on this stock. Also included in this asset category is stock acquired incident to foreclosure on loans, foreign stock held for investment purposes, and the bank's minority interest in subsidiary companies.

Trading Account Securities

Trading account securities are those held for resale to other banks and the public. IRS regulations require that these securities be carried at market value in lieu of book value. Appreciation or depreciation in market value is reported as an ordinary gain or loss on the income statement. At the close of 1977, insured commercial banks held $6.4 billion or 0.6 percent of their assets in trading account securities.

Federal Funds Sold and Securities Purchased Under Agreement to Resell

Federal funds sold are excess reserves that banks lend to each other, usually on an overnight basis. The sale of federal funds is the primary way banks utilize excess funds on a daily basis to maximize income from investable assets. Most purchases and sales of federal funds are effected on the books of Federal Reserve Banks; hence, the origin of the word "federal" in federal funds. The rate charged for federal funds is the *federal fund rate* and is a sensitive measure of the supply and demand for investable funds.

Securities purchased under agreement to resell represent another temporary use of excess funds. Under this arrangement, banks enter into an agreement with another commercial bank, government security dealer, foreign agency, or any other firm, institution, or organization to purchase a given amount of Treasury or agency obligations and to resell them after a specified time at a certain price. With this technique, the bank is guaranteed a fixed-return, and the selling institution acquires funds to make adjustments in inventory or for other purposes. At the end of 1977, insured commercial banks held $49.7 billion or 4.4 percent of their assets in the form of federal funds sold and securities purchased under agreement to resell.

Loans

It is often said that loans are the highest and best use of bank funds. This is because loans made in the local economy stimulate growth in employment, income, deposits, and—eventually—profits for the bank. Table 1-2 contains a list of the major types of bank loans along with amounts outstanding at insured commercial banks for selected dates between 1970 and 1977.

Real Estate Loans. This loan category includes permanent loans to finance homes, factories, office buildings, and retail outlets, as well as temporary construction financing of these facilities. Traditionally,

Table 1-2.   Loans Outstanding at Insured Commercial Banks, Selected Years, 1970–1977 (Billions of Dollars).

	YEAR ENDING DECEMBER 31				
	1970	1972	1974	1976	1977
Real estate loans	73.1	99.1	131.8	150.9	176.9
Loans to domestic banks and foreign banks	2.6	6.1	10.1	9.4	10.4
Loans to other financial institutions	15.8	23.4	35.1	26.4	26.3
Loans to brokers and dealers in securities	6.2	11.2	5.2	11.1	12.8
Other loans for purchasing or carrying securities	3.5	4.5	4.0	4.0	4.3
Loans to farmers (excluding loans on real estate)	11.2	14.3	18.2	23.3	25.7
Commercial and industrial loans (including open market paper)	112.2	132.5	184.2	178.8	195.4
Other loans to individuals	66.0	87.6	103.7	118.9	140.3
All other loans	7.7	10.2	14.1	14.7	15.7
Total loans	298.3	388.9	506.4	537.5	607.8
	PERCENTAGE DISTRIBUTION				
Real estate loans	24.5	25.5	26.0	28.1	29.1
Loans to domestic banks and foreign banks	.9	1.6	2.0	1.7	1.7
Loans to other financial institutions	5.3	6.0	6.9	4.9	4.3
Loans to brokers and dealers in securities	2.1	2.9	1.0	2.1	2.1
Other loans for purchasing and carrying securities	1.2	1.2	.8	.7	0.7
Loans to farmers (excluding loans on real estate)	3.8	3.7	3.6	4.3	4.2
Commercial and industrial loans (including open market paper)	37.6	34.1	36.4	33.3	32.1
Other loans to individuals	22.1	22.5	20.5	22.1	23.1
All other loans	2.6	2.6	2.8	2.7	2.6
Total	100.0	100.0	100.0	100.0	100.0

Source: FDIC, *Annual Reports* and *Federal Reserve Bulletin.*

banks avoided real estate lending because it was believed that banks should make only short-term commercial loans to businesses. Short-term lending was dictated by the bank's deposit liabilities, which historically have been primarily short-term; i.e., demand deposits. Since World War II, however, longer-term sources of bank funds, such as time and savings deposits have increased sharply and now comprise almost 60 percent of total bank deposits. Longer term, more stable sources of funds have enabled banks to reach out for longer-term, higher yielding assets such as real estate loans. As shown in Table 1-2, on December 31, 1977, real estate loans made up 29.1 percent of the total loans held by insured commercial banks. On the same date, in California, where time and savings deposits comprise 62.9 percent of total deposits, real estate loans made up 33.5 percent of total bank loans.

Loans to Domestic and Foreign Banks. This category includes federal funds sold, transactions with an initial maturity beyond one day, and other loans to domestic and foreign banks. Interbank loans are a convenient and efficient short-term use of funds for banks with weak loan demand.

Loans to Other Financial Institutions. This category includes loans to finance companies, savings and loan associations, life insurance companies, casualty insurance companies, mutual savings banks, and credit unions. Loans to sales and consumer finance companies account for the bulk of this category. Finance companies, in turn, lend to many customers who do not qualify for bank loans.

Loans to Brokers and Dealers. Banks make loans on securities to brokers and dealers, who finance their own security transactions or the purchase or sale of securities on margin for their customers.

Other Loans to Purchase/Carry Securities. This category represents funds advanced to individuals and non-brokers and dealers for the purpose of purchasing and carrying securities.

Loans to Farmers In spite of the many federally assisted credit institutions that lend almost exclusively to farmers, banks still are an important source of loans to farmers. These loans finance current expenditures, equipment, cattle, and a myriad of other items and needs.

Commercial and Industrial Loans. Commercial and industrial loans represent the largest loan category, accounting for 32.1 percent of the loan portfolio of insured banks at the end of 1977. Commercial and industrial loans may be classified either as short-term loans or *term loans* (those with an original maturity of one year or more). Prior to the Great Depression, most bankers considered making short-term loans to businesses their primary role. The theory was that since bank liabilities essentially were short-term, bank assets primarily should be short-term. Moreover, most bankers believed that the only good short-term loans were business loans because they directly led to the creation of jobs and income in the economy. Consumer loans were thought to be "unproductive" because they did not lead directly to the creation of jobs and income.

For what purposes do businesses borrow on a short-term basis from banks? Essentially, most short-term business loans are working capital loans. Businesses use the funds for purchasing inventory and raw materials, for financing accounts receivable, and for many other short-term cash needs. Many manufacturing businesses have a definite seasonal pattern to their operation; that is, during a certain time of the year, the firm is involved primarily with manufacturing its product. During this period, the firm is a cash user and needs short-term financing. During another time of the year, the firm is involved primarily with selling the product and, hence, is generating cash. During the selling period, the firm will be paying off its short-term bank debt. A doll company with manufacturing concentrated in the spring and summer, while sales take place in the early fall, is an example of a seasonal business with this cash flow pattern.

Banks make term loans to businesses primarily to finance the acquisition of capital goods such as plants and equipment. Other uses of term loans include financing the acquisition of another firm, or providing permanent working capital necessitated by growth in sales.

Loans to Individuals. At the close of 1977, insured banks had 23.1 percent of their loan portfolios in "loan to individuals." This loan category includes automobile loans, credit card loans, loans to purchase mobile homes and other consumer durables, loans for residential repair and modernization, and other installment and single-payment loans to finance personal expenditures. Needless to say, loans to individuals are no longer considered "unproductive." Besides being some of the highest yielding loans in a bank's portfolio, loans to individuals enable goods and services to be purchased and thus stimulate business to invest in new plants and equipment, leading to more jobs and income in the community.

Since 1976, only net loans are shown as bank assets. *Net loans* are total loans less unearned income and reserve for possible loan losses. *Unearned income* represents future income on loans. For example, if a person signs a one-year note at a bank for $1,000 and the bank discounts the interest at 8 percent, the bank's total loan at inception is $1,000, but the net loan is $920, after excluding $80 in unearned income.

The *provision for possible loan losses* represents the valuation position of a bank's bad debt reserve. There are three parts to the bad debt reserve: (1) valuation portion, (2) contingency portion, and (3) deferred tax portion. The valuation portion or provision for possible loan losses is the portion subtracted from total loans. The provision for possible loan losses is increased by charges to income and decreased by loan losses charged off. Under IRS regulations, banks may build up the "provision for loan losses" until it equals 1.2 percent of eligible loans. In other words, banks can create a tax free reserve to absorb future loan losses.

The contingency portion represents transfers from equity capital to reserve for bad debts. That is, a bank can create a larger reserve for bad debts than is provided for by charges to income. The contingency portion is shown under the equity capital of the balance sheet as a "reserve for contingencies and other capital reserves."

The deferred tax portion represents the tax effect on the difference between the deduction for loan losses claimed for income tax purposes pursuant to IRS rulings and the "provision for possible loan losses" claimed for financial reporting purposes. In other words, the deferred tax portion is the result of a timing difference between the bookkeeping entries made for income tax accounting and those made for regular financial reporting. The deferred tax portion is included under "other liabilities."

Direct Lease Financing

Direct lease financing includes the outstanding balances of all types of leases on property acquired by the bank for purposes of lease financing. In recent years, many banks have started purchasing and leasing all kinds of property, including ocean-going tankers, airplanes, construction equipment, and medical and dental equipment. Several banks in farming communities have leased bulls to local farmers for breeding purposes. Leasing offers banks a return on invested funds that usually is somewhat higher than on loans. At the close of 1977, insured banks had $5.8 billion in direct lease financing.

Bank Premises, Furniture, and Fixtures, and Other Assets Representing Bank Premises

This item represents the book value, less depreciation reserves, of all bank premises and furniture and fixtures. Included are "leasehold improvements," such as partitions and walls placed in leased facilities, buildings erected on leased property, resurfacing and other improvements on parking lots, and vaults, fixed machinery, and other equipment. Although bank premises and furniture and fixtures are not assets that directly create an income stream, they nevertheless are important because they enable the bank to acquire earning assets.

Real Estate Owned Other Than Bank Premises

This item represents the book value, less depreciation reserves, of all real estate other than bank premises actually owned by the bank and its consolidated subsidiaries. One item included under this heading is real estate acquired through foreclosure. The amount of this asset on a bank's books is an indication of the quality of loan management.

Investments in Unconsolidated Subsidiaries and "Associated Companies"

This asset category includes the total investment in majority-owned subsidiaries such as domestic commercial banks and foreign and domestic companies not meeting the tests for required consolidation and for which the bank does not exercise the optional consolidation provision.

Customers Liability to Bank on Acceptances Outstanding

In the course of financing exports and imports, a bank accepts drafts drawn on the bank by individuals and firms directing payment of a specified sum of money to the order of a designated party or to the bearer at a specified future date. By its "acceptance" written on the draft, the bank commits itself to make the payment as directed. The bank is willing to make this commitment because the individual or firm receiving the goods agrees to pay the bank in the future. This commitment by the customer to pay is the asset item listed here. The bank's obligation for the accepted draft is listed on the liability side of the statement of condition as "Acceptances Executed by or for Account of this Bank and Outstanding." Usually, the asset and liability amounts for acceptances are identical.

Other Assets

"Other assets" is a catch-all category for all assets not large enough to warrant a separate line item. Examples of "other assets" are securities borrowed, the net amount due from foreign branches, income earned or accrued but not collected, prepaid expenses, cash items not in process of collection, and balances with savings and loan associations.

BANK LIABILITIES

Deposits are the principal source of insured bank funds; hence, they are the largest bank liability. In 1950, deposits comprised 92.0 percent of total funds sources, with equity capital and other liabilities providing 6.8 percent and 1.2 percent, respectively. By 1977, deposits had declined to 81.7 percent of total sources of funds, while equity capital, subordinated notes and debentures, and other liabilities accounted for 7.0 percent, 0.5 percent, and 10.8 percent, respectively. In the late 1960's, the advent of *liability management*, a process designed to locate and acquire funds at the lowest possible cost, was largely responsible for the increase in nondeposit liabilities as sources of funds.

Demand Deposits of Individuals, Partnerships, and Corporations

Prior to 1965, demand deposits of individuals, partnerships, and corporations (IPC) exceeded time and savings deposits. With improved cash management techniques, the ubiquitous use of credit cards, and the incentive of high interest rates on time and savings deposits and money market instruments, business and individuals have economized greatly on the amount of IPC demand deposits needed. Between 1970 and 1977, GNP rose 92.3 percent, while IPC demand deposits increased 56.8 percent. By 1977, IPC demand deposits comprised 30.9 percent of total deposits.

Of total IPC demand deposits, about 61.2 percent are owned by businesses, with 38.8 percent held by "others." A significant percentage of total business deposits are held in banks with deposits of $100 million or more. This is primarily because large corporations, which account for the bulk of the business deposits, have to go to large banks to accommodate their credit needs and, as part of the loan agreement, usually agree to keep their corporate deposits at the lending bank.

Time and Savings Deposits of Individuals, Partnerships, and Corporations

IPC time and savings deposits take three primary forms: (1) savings deposits, (2) time deposits, open account, and (3) time certificates of deposit. *Savings Deposits* have no specified maturity and no contractual provisions that require the depositor to give written notice of an intention to withdraw funds. Customers eligible to hold savings deposits include individuals, nonprofit organizations, government agencies and corporations, state and political subdivisions, and international organizations.

Time deposit contracts are distinguished from demand and savings accounts by provisions specifying maturity or other withdrawal conditions. A *time deposit, open account* (TDOA) is a deposit, other than a time certificate of deposit, with respect to which there is in force a written contract with the depositor that neither the whole nor any part of such deposit may be withdrawn, by check or otherwise, prior to the date of maturity, which shall not be less than 30 days after the date of the deposit, or prior to the expiration of the period of notice, which must be given by the depositor in writing not less than 30 days in advance of withdrawal. If funds in a TDOA are withdrawn prior to maturity, the depositor must forfeit three months' interest, and interest on the amount withdrawn is reduced to the rate on savings deposits. Banks have been highly successful in attracting TDOA's. The "golden passbook savings account" that is advertised extensively around the country is a TDOA.

A *time certificate of deposit* (CD) is a deposit evidenced by a negotiable or non-negotiable instrument (the certificate) that provides on its face that the amount of each deposit is payable either (1) on a certain date, specified in the instrument, not less than 30 days after date of deposit; or (2) at the expiration of a specified period, not less than 30 days after the date of the instrument; or (3) upon written notice to be given not less than 30 days before the date of repayment.

Negotiable CD's are denominated in amounts ranging from $100,000 to $100 million, with a $1 million face value as a standard trading unit. The most popular maturities lie in the six-months to one-year range. The principal purchasers of negotiable CD's are large corporations, state and local governments, and wealthy individuals. At the close of 1977, the volume of outstanding negotiable CD's stood at $154.0 billion. On the same date, IPC time and savings deposits of all types totaled $475.0 billion or 51.5 percent of total deposits. Between 1970 and 1977, IPC time and savings deposits increased 126.6 percent and accounted for 59.9 percent of the total increase in deposits.

The shift in deposit structure from demand to time and savings deposits has several important implications for bank asset management. The lengthening maturity of deposits has permitted banks to make longer term commercial and industrial loans and increase real estate loans. Moreover, investment strategy has changed to emphasize longer-term municipals.

Deposits of the U.S. Government

U.S. Government deposits represent funds held in Treasury tax and loan (TT & L) accounts. Any bank is eligible to receive TT & L deposits if it qualifies through the district Federal Reserve Bank. Individuals, businesses, and governmental units remit federal tax payments of all types through TT & L accounts. When banks purchase Treasury securities, they sometimes pay for them by simply crediting their TT & L accounts. As needed, these funds are shifted to the Treasury's General Account at the Federal Reserve Bank. The Treasury pays its bills out of this general account. At the end of 1977, U.S. Government deposits in TT & L accounts totaled $8.2 billion.

Deposits of States and Political Subdivisions

States and their subdivisions held $75.8 billion in total deposits at the close of 1977. Of this total, approximately three-fourths was in time and savings deposits, with the remainder in demand accounts. As a source of funds, state and local governments rank second only to individuals, partnerships, and corporations. This distribution is the result of the frequency of revenue receipts. For example, local property taxes are paid once a year, while disbursements usually are made smoothly over the year. County treasurers take advantage of this lag by holding a large proportion of their deposits in interest-bearing form.

Deposits of Foreign Governments and Official Institutions

These deposits include those of central banks, foreign development banks, treasuries, exchange control offices, stabilization funds, and International institutions such as the International Bank for Reconstruction and Development and the Inter-American Development Bank. At the end of 1977, foreign official deposits totaled $9.9 billion.

Deposits of Banks in Foreign Countries

This deposit category includes all deposits of foreign commercial banks, savings banks, discount houses, and other similar foreign institutions.

Deposits of Commercial Banks

As pointed out earlier, interbank deposits serve two primary functions: (1) as legal reserves for non-member banks and (2) as compensation for services rendered, primarily check clearing. At the end of 1977, these deposits stood at $47.3 billion, and were the third largest source of funds.

Certified and Officer's Checks, Letters of Credit, and Traveler's checks

A *certified check* is a regular check drawn by a customer on his bank and stamped "certified" or "guaranteed." An *officer's check* or *cashier's check* is an order, drawn by a bank officer, to pay on demand. A *letter of credit* authorizes specified individuals to draw drafts on the bank payable on demand. A *travelers' check* is an engraved instrument that gives the holder the right to demand money at any time. Banks charge their customers a small fee for selling them any of these instruments and immediately deduct the amount of these obligations issued from the customer's account. Because these instruments are in the nature of short-term claims, they are classified as demand deposits.

BANK NONDEPOSIT LIABILITIES

Bank nondeposit liabilities at the end of 1977 comprised 10.8 percent of the total sources of bank funds. In the years ahead, it is likely that banks will rely increasingly on nondeposit sources of funds.

Federal Funds Purchased and Securities Sold
Under Agreements to Repurchase

Federal funds purchased are excess reserves borrowed by one bank from another, typically on an overnight basis. The word "federal" stems from the fact that most "fed funds" transactions take place on the books of the Federal Reserve. In recent years, the term "federal funds purchased" has been broadened to include funds transferred among banks on the books of commercial banks. Securities sold under agreements to repurchase ("Repos") are bank liabilities representing a bank obligation to buy back securities sold to a dealer or another bank. Repos enable banks to acquire reserves on a temporary basis without liquidating part of their security holdings. Today, the principal way that banks acquire temporary funds is through fed funds and repo transactions. The growing significance of fed funds and repo transactions is readily apparent in Table 1-1. Between 1970 and 1977, this liability category increased from $16.6 billion to $82.8 billion and accounted for 7.3 percent of total funds sources at the end of 1977.

Liabilities for Borrowed Money

This bank liability includes funds borrowed on the bank's own promissory notes; on notes and bills rediscounted (including commodity drafts rediscounted); on loans sold with the reporting bank's endorsement or guarantee; or any other instruments given for the purpose of borrowing money. Also included are overdrawn amounts with other domestic and foreign banks, loans from Federal Reserve Banks, and loans sold under formal agreements to repurchase.

Mortgage Indebtedness

This liability includes amounts of mortgages, liens, or encumbrances on bank premises or other real estate owned for which the bank or its consolidated subsidiaries are liable.

Acceptances Outstanding

Unmatured drafts and bills of exchange accepted by banks, less the amount of such acceptances acquired through discount or purchase, comprise this liability category. "Acceptances outstanding" is the companion account to the asset account, "customers' liability on acceptances outstanding." For most banks, the acceptance asset account matches the acceptance liability account. This is true because when a bank accepts a draft or bill of exchange, it creates a liability and also acquires an asset, the obligation of a customer to pay the bank an equal amount.

Other Liabilities

Some items under the "other liability" class include the "net amount due from foreign branches," "income earned or accrued but not collected," "prepaid expenses," and "cash items not in the process of collection."

BANK SUBORDINATED NOTES AND DEBENTURES

In 1962, the Comptroller of the Currency, James J. Saxon, ruled that banks should be able to have access to the money and capital markets to which industrial corporations have access. As a result of this ruling, banks began to raise funds through the issurance of notes and debentures. At the close of 1977, $5.7 billion was outstanding.

In addition to being a source of funds, notes and debentures also benefit a bank's depositors and other claimholders, because in case of large loan losses or even bank failure, notes and debentures are subordinated to the claims of depositors and the holders of other liabilities. Notes and debentures either may be convertible or non-convertible into the shares of the bank.

BANK EQUITY CAPITAL

Equity capital represents the owner's claim on assets and is the sum of preferred and common stock outstanding, surplus, undivided profits, and reserve for contingencies and other capital reserves.

Preferred Stock

Preferred stock is a very minor source of funds. At the end of 1977, there was only $79 million in preferred stock outstanding. Much of this preferred was issued in bank merger transactions under circumstances whereby the merging bank did not want to issue common stock to the shareholders of the bank being taken over. If common stock is issued in a merger, control by existing owners is diluted. The principal disadvantage of issuing preferred stock is that dividends on it are non-deductible for income tax purposes. Investors find preferred stock unattractive because the appreciation potential is limited.

Common Stock, Surplus, and Undivided Profits

The amount listed under a bank's *common stock* account is equal to the number of shares outstanding times the par value of the stock. A bank issues common stock when it is organized, if it pays a stock dividend or declares a stock split, and sometimes in a merger with another bank.

The *surplus account* reflects the sale of common stock at a premium over the par value and transfers from the undivided profits account. A bank's common stock and surplus sometimes are referred to as "permanent capital." Banks must apply to their regulatory authority to increase or decrease surplus. Surplus is increased by decreasing undivided profits. The only time surplus might be decreased is when loan losses or any other asset write down is so large it wipes out the reserve for loan losses and undivided profits, thereby causing the bank to invade surplus. Several banks had to do this because of large losses suffered during the 1973–1975 recession and the associated collapse in the real estate market.

The bank *undivided profits* account might be considered as "temporary profits" and is similar to the earned surplus account of non-bank businesses. Accrued profits and losses are credited and debited to this account. Dividends paid to shareholders are debited to this account.

At the end of 1977, common stock, surplus, and undivided profits totaled $79.1 billion or 7.0 percent of total sources of funds. As shall be discussed in detail in Chapter 3, the primary function of bank equity capital is to demonstrate the ability to absorb unanticipated losses on the asset side. When a bank has to write off an asset such as a loan, shareholders lose because they must give up an equal claim on assets.

CONCLUDING OBSERVATIONS

In this chapter, we have looked at the bank statement of condition, a document that reveals at one moment in time the schedule of assets such as cash in vault, loans, and securities. Equal to these assets are the claims of the non-owners, principally depositors, and the claims of shareholders. A comparison of statements of condition over time reveals changes not only in the total quantity of assets and claims but in composition as well. The statement of condition is the basic bank document used in the analysis of bank liquidity and bank capital adequacy, the respective subjects of Chapters 2 and 3.

2
Liquidity Analysis

In Chapter 1, we looked into the nature of major bank assets, liabilities, and capital accounts. Bank assets are "things owned." Bank liabilities represent non-owner claims on assets, while capital represents owner claims on assets. This chapter deals with liquidity analysis and primarily involves the evaluation of a bank's ability to pay its non-owner claims as promised. Specifically, we shall (1) discuss the nature of bank liquidity, (2) examine the purposes, problems, and perspectives of liquidity analysis, and (3) set forth techniques of liquidity analysis that might be employed by a bank's management and by "outsiders" such as depositors, creditors, shareholders, and potential investors.

INTRODUCTION TO BANK LIQUIDITY

The Banker's Dilemma: Liquidity versus Profitability

Financial institutions such as banks acquire funds by making promises to pay money in the future. Most of these promises stipulate that payment will be made at the end of a certain period of time, as in the case of CD's with fixed maturities. Banks, however, promise to redeem demand deposit liabilities on demand. To prepare for the contingency that holders of demand deposits, currently due time deposits, and other liabilities might all request their funds at the same time, banks could hold cash assets equal to 100 percent of these claims. But since cash assets yield a zero return, banks would have to charge demand depositors prohibitively high service fees in order to earn a sufficient income to pay expenses and a fair return on shareholders' capital. Obviously, such a course of action would be implausible because other financial intermediaries offer alternative means of storing and transferring funds.

At the other extreme, in an effort to maximize income, banks could acquire only high-yielding, long-term assets and hope that the daily inflow of new funds would be greater than, or equal to, the daily requests for deposit redemption and loans and the amount of current liabilities due. It is highly unlikely, of course, that the inflows and outflows of funds always will balance. Realistically, the best strategy for banks to follow lies somewhere between the two extremes.

Banks strive to find the optimal balance between liquidity and profitability in the management of their assets and liabilities. In the ordering of priorities, meeting deposit and other liability claims is a necessary condition for staying in business. If a bank's depositors and other liability holders do not have confidence that the claims can be met, they will refuse to deposit or lend funds to the bank. The acquisition of deposits and other funds, of course, is a necessary condition for the expansion of loans and investments beyond the amount permitted by the use of capital only. Maintaining adequate liquidity is the most important constraint upon a bank's primary objective—maximizing shareholder wealth.

Some Important Bank Liquidity Concepts

Before we examine some techniques of liquidity analysis, it will be helpful to define and explain some important bank liquidity concepts.

An *individual bank's liquidity* is its ability to meet deposit withdrawals, maturing liabilities, and loan requests without delay. A bank is "liquid" if (1) it holds cash assets (cash-in-vault, balances at the Federal Reserve Bank, or balances at correspondent banks) equal to its expected liquidity demands; (2) it holds less than this amount of cash assets, but it also holds other assets (primarily securities) that can be exchanged for cash assets without delay and without suffering undue loss of full market value; or (3) it has the ability to acquire cash assets through the creation of liabilities such as federal funds purchases or securities sold under agreements to repurchase.

Liquidity management involves the continuous estimation of, and provision for, a bank's immediate, short-term or seasonal, as well as long-term (cyclical and secular) cash requirements. Immediate cash needs are specified by legal and working reserve requirements. *Legal reserve requirements* are the Federal Reserve's regulation (for member banks) or a state's regulation (for non-member banks) that banks hold specific assets called *legal reserves* equal to a percentage of their deposits and certain other liabilities; e.g., short-term commercial paper sold by the holding company that owns the bank. The Fed specifies that member banks hold cash-in-vault and/or balances with Federal Reserve banks as legal reserves. State reserve requirements vary from state to state with respect to both the type of assets that qualify as legal reserves and the percentage of deposit and other liabilities that must be held in this form. Most states specify that cash-in-vault and correspondent balances are legal reserves. *Working reserve requirements* are a bank's need for cash assets to meet the daily demand for currency and coin and to meet the balance requirements to compensate correspondent banks for services rendered. Working reserve requirements are over and above the bank's legal reserve requirements. Cash assets held to meet legal and working reserve requirements comprise the bank's *money position.*

A bank's *short-term or seasonal liquidity requirements* are those that vary from month-to-month and tend to recur regularly from year-to-year. *Cyclical and secular liquidity requirements* are those related to the level of economic and financial activity in the economy and the absolute growth in deposits and loans. Sources of bank liquidity needs may be classifed as follows: (1) the money position, (2) short-term or seasonal, and (3) long-term or cyclical and secular.

Sources of Bank Liquidity Requirements

The Money Position. A bank's need for cash assets in its money position arises primarily from the reserve requirements of bank regulatory authorities, correspondent balance requirements, and the need not to be embarrassed in the daily business of cashing and paying checks and liabilities when due. Reserve requirements are enforced by the regulatory authorities, while correspondent banks monitor daily the balance requirements that have been negotiated as compensation for services performed. With respect to meeting customers' currency and coin needs, seldom does bank management have inadequate cash-in-vault. If there is a shortage, it is a simple matter to obtain currency and coin from another bank. Finally, the daily volume of checks paid on a bank usually is closely balanced with checks received on other banks. Most banks adjust for any net difference in check clearing by adjusting the amount of fed funds bought and sold.

It often surprises banking students to learn that a bank's minimum holdings of cash-in-vault balances with the Fed and that correspondent balances really are "illiquid assets" because they are unavailable to meet deposit withdrawals, maturing liabilities, and new credit demands. The exception is when a depositor redeems his deposits, and the bank's required reserves decline by the amount of the reserve ratio times the deposit withdrawal; in this case, a fraction of the deposit withdrawal is met from cash assets in the money position. However, the thrust of bank liquidity analysis is concerned not with having cash assets on a daily basis to meet legal reserve, correspondent bank, and daily transactions requirements, but with a bank's ability to meet deposit withdrawals, maturing liabilities, and credit demands and commitments over two time horizons: (1) the short-run, a period of one year when seasonal factors dominate, and (2) the long-run, a period during which the cycle in economic and financial activity and the secular growth in deposits and loans are the primary determinants of liquidity needs. Management of the money position will "take care of itself," if a bank's liquidity plans take into account these short- and long-run factors.

Short-term Liquidity Needs. Short-term liquidity needs are those that result from seasonal and random fluctuations over the course of a year in the demand for funds. We may classify these short-term requirements as needs for deposit liquidity, loan liquidity, and liability liquidity.

A bank's short-term need for *deposit liquidity* depends largely on its location, the maturity schedule of its time and savings deposits, and the payment schedules and practices of its large demand deposit holders. A bank located in the Florida citrus belt would have a different seasonal deposit profile than would a bank located in a tobacco farming community in South Carolina. Deposits in the former would tend to rise in winter, then stabilize and decline toward fall; deposits in the latter would tend to fall in winter and spring and rise in late summer and fall, when the crop is sold. Seasonal deposit fluctuations of this sort may be readily identified by statistical analysis of the monthly total deposits series.

At first glance, the rising proportion of time and savings deposits would seem to reduce a bank's short-term liquidity needs. This is because these deposits traditionally have been quite stable. This is true for savings type deposits, including TDOA's. However, CD's are a source of both stability and instability with respect to planning short-term liquidity needs. Because maturity dates are known, banks can plan short-term liquidity needs better. Maturities of one year or more mean that these deposits cannot create a liquidity need within the one-year planning horizon. On the other hand, CD's maturing within one year create uncertainty because the bank cannot be sure of the portion that will be renewed. As most bankers learned in the tight money period of 1973–1974, when money market rates rise well above interest rates that banks may pay or are willing to pay on CD's, many CD holders cash in their claims and move into higher-yielding money market instruments.

Tax and dividend payment requirements of large corporations are a chief source of short-term liquidity needs. When quarterly corporate income taxes and dividends are due, many banks experience sizable runoff in demand deposits. For example, on December 10, 1977, General Motors paid almost $863 million in dividends to its common stockholders. Within a week, the bulk of these checks were presented to the bank holding GM's dividend account.

A bank's need for *loan liquidity* ordinarily parallels its need for deposit liquidity, since borrowers usually draw down their deposits before they seek loan accommodations. Thus, the same institutional arrangements and seasonal influences that bear on deposit liquidity determine loan liquidity requirements. During recent tight money periods, many corporations had to borrow heavily to meet quarterly tax payments and other cash needs. In fact, the dollar amounts and number of corporations involved were so large that the financial press started reporting how well banks were able to meet the demand for loans around tax-payment dates.

Besides the need to meet tax payments, each industry has its own special seasonal borrowing needs. Firms in the tobacco industry tend to increase their borrowing during late summer and fall, when they have to purchase the current year's tobacco crop. Retail businesses typically borrow in late summer and early fall in order to purchase their Christmas inventories. The seasonal peak in the sales of automobiles, appliances, and television sets during fall tends to coincide with the seasonal demand for bank loans by sales finance companies, who often finance the purchase of these items. Construction companies have a great demand for loans during the spring and summer months because of the seasonal peak in residential building. The agricultural sector, of course, has its unique seasonal borrowing needs. To the extent that these loan demands cannot be met from loan repayments and increases in deposits, the bank must have adequate short-term liquidity reserves.

Long-term Liquidity Needs. Long-term liquidity needs have their origin primarily in the cyclical nature of economic activity. Unlike short-term liquidity requirements—which tend to be repetitive because of the nature of our tax system, quarterly dividend payments patterns, the weather, and the celebration of holidays—cyclical liquidity needs are rather unpredictable. Since World War II, the U.S. economy has experienced six major recessions: (1) 1948–1949, (2) 1953–1954, (3) 1957–1958, (4) 1960–1961, (5) 1969–1970, and (6) 1973–1975. The periods of economic expansion that separated these recessions varied considerably in length and intensity. Moreover, some economists believe that the Federal Reserve's monetary policy is a contributing factor to both the expansionary and contractionary phases of the business cycle. Therefore, in the analysis of a bank's liquidity, it is important to know the direction in economic activity and the probable course of monetary policy.

According to modern liquidity theory, banks experience their greatest need for liquidity during periods of economic expansion and not during periods of slow growth or recession,[1] when liquidity tends to increase as required reserves fall due to the decline of deposits and loans. Moreover, it is unlikely that the banking system will experience another severe liquidity panic similar to that in the Great Depression. There are several factors substantiating this viewpoint: (1) the establishment of the FDIC; (2) the Fed's greater knowledge of the art of central banking; (3) the federal government's commitment to full employment; and (4) the improved quality of bank loan portfolios (in comparison to those in the late 1920's) because of better trained lending officers and more stringent bank examinations.

During the expansion phase of the business cycle, loan demand usually rises very sharply. Most of this increase represents funds advanced to businesses to finance new plants and equipment, inventories, and accounts receivable. Individual banks risk losing accounts when they cannot accommodate the loan requests of their established customers. Moreover, because the Fed usually attempts to restrict the growth of deposits during the last phases of an economic expansion, banks ordinarily cannot rely on this source of funds to finance an expansion of loans. In order to meet these loan requests, banks must have enough short-term securities that can be sold with little or no loss, or they must have the ability to borrow funds in sufficient volume through various liability management techniques to fulfill their customers' credit needs.[2]

TECHNIQUES OF LIQUIDITY ANALYSIS FOR MANAGEMENT

Difficulties involved

The previous section provided the conceptual and theoretical foundation for understanding the sources of bank liquidity requirements. However, there is a considerable gap between the theoretical understanding of bank liquidity needs and the state of the art of measuring

---

[1]Much of this discussion is based on G. Walter Woodworth's article, "Bank Liquidity Management," in *The Bankers Magazine,* Autumn 1967, pp. 66–78.

[2]Some primary liability management techniques include the issuance of CD's, the purchase of federal funds, the borrowing of Eurodollars, and borrowing from the Federal Reserve.

a bank's liquidity. The principal difficulty encountered in liquidity analysis is that a judgment must be made in the present about a bank's ability to meet its liquidity needs in the future. Short-run influences, such as seasonal factors, are fairly predictable; however, long-run influences originating from cycles in economic and financial activity are difficult to estimate. For example, few experts foresaw the 1973–1974 credit crunch and the severe decline in bank liquidity that took place. The failure of a number of banks during this period, including Franklin National Bank with assets of $3.6 billion in October, 1974, was primarily a result of liquidity pressures. At the time of this writing (spring 1978), economists are divided on the outlook for 1979 and 1980. Some predict continued economic expansion, while others foresee a major recession. Bank liquidity planning would differ quite markedly, depending on whose forecast is followed.

A Three-Step Liquidity Planning and Analysis System

Even for management with access to internal data, liquidity planning and analysis is not a simple, mechanical task. Judgment is involved at every juncture. Moreover, a liquidity planning and analysis system must be practical and workable. Recently, Daniel J. Kaufman, Jr. and David R. Lee, of the Winters National Bank and Trust Company in Dayton, Ohio, proposed a system that meets these criteria and is very conservative in approach.[3]

Before examining the steps in this system, Figure 2-1 should be studied. This chart classifies assets as liquid or non-liquid; liabilities and capital are classified as reliable or volatile. Each account is expressed as a percentage of the average balance expected over the bank's planning cycle (usually 12 months). In essence, the system proposed by Kaufman and Lee involves identification of a bank's potential needs for liquidity and a comparison of these needs with the bank's holdings of liquid assets. For convenience, the explanation will be divided into three parts.

[3]Daniel J. Kaufman, Jr. and David R. Lee, "Planning Liquidity: A Practical Approach," Bank Administration Institute, *The Magazine of Bank Administration*, February, 1977, pp. 55–63.

Figure 2-1. Sample National Bank Detail Report

ASSETS	LIQUID ASSETS		NON-LIQUID ASSETS		AVERAGE BALANCE
	%	$ (000)	%	$ (000)	$ (000)
CASH ASSETS					
Cash including reserves	6.4	1,198	93.6	17,517	18,715
Items in the process of collection	2.8	346	97.2	12,005	12,351
Total cash assets	5.0	1,544	95.0	29,522	31,066
INVESTMENTS					
U.S. Government securities	43.2	12,237	56.8	16,091	28,328
Tax exempt securities	30.7	11,164	69.3	25,201	36,365
Other securities	37.4	358	62.6	600	958
Fed funds sold	100.0	6,556	0	0	6,556
Total investments	42.0	30,315	58.0	41,892	72,207
LOANS					
Commercial loans	-7.3	-5,363	107.3	78,819	73,456
Mortgage and construction	5.0	2,350	95.0	44,662	47,012
Installment loans	7.4	2,188	93.6	27,382	29,570
Charge card	0	0	100.0	4,986	4,986
Overdraft loans	0	0	100.0	1,571	1,571
Total loans	-0.5	- 825	100.5	157,420	156,595
Premises and equipment	0	0	100.0	4,165	4,165
Other assets	27.2	1,169	72.8	3,131	4,300
Total assets	12.0	32,203*	88.0	236,130	268,333

LIABILITIES AND CAPITAL	VOLATILE FUNDS		RELIABLE FUNDS		AVERAGE BALANCE
	%	$ (000)	%	$ (000)	$ (000)
Total deposits	6.4	14,063	93.6	205,674	219,737
Fed funds purchased	100.0	17,295	0	0	17,295
Other borrowings	100.0	14	0	0	14
Other liabilities	8.8	898	91.2	9,313	10,211
Total liabilities	13.0	32,270	87.0	214,987	247,257
Shareholders' equity	0	0	100.0	21,076	21,076
Total liabilities and equity	12.0	32,270	88.0	236,063	268,333

*Net liquid assets.

Source: Adapted from article by Daniel J. Kaufman, Jr. and David R. Lee, "Planning Liquidity: A Practical Approach," Bank Administration Institute, *The Magazine of Bank Administration,* February, 1977, p. 57.

Part I: Classify Liabilities and Capital Either as Reliable or Volatile Sources of Funds. First and foremost, a bank is concerned with its ability to meet deposit withdrawals and maturing liabilities. The initial step, then, is identify potential sources of liquidity needs eminating from the liabilities and capital side of the balance sheet.

Beginning with deposits, the objective is to classify deposits either as reliable or volatile sources of funds. *Reliable funds* might be considered "bedrock" funds that the bank does not expect to lose. *Volatile funds* are those with a high expectation of loss. There are two schools of thought as to how to make this determination. One viewpoint is to examine each major deposit category (demand, regular savings, CD's, etc.) and determine what percentage of the average balance in each account and in each deposit category is reliable or volatile. Proponents of this view argue that a detailed examination enables the bank to utilize knowledge about individual accounts that might be overlooked if only total deposits were considered. The other viewpoint is that individual account analysis does not take into consideration that a decline in one deposit account might be offset by an increase in another. For example, funds received from a maturing CD might be transferred to a regular savings account. According to this viewpoint, the sum of the volatile elements in each individual deposit account is usually greater than the volatility of total deposits. The later approach is favored here for the reasons given above and because time and cost considerations make individual account analysis prohibitive. However, banks faced with a heavy schedule of maturing CD's, during a period of rising interest rates, may want to consider account by account the likelihood of renewal.

To estimate the percentage of total deposits that might be considered volatile, first analyze fluctuations in total deposits during the most recent phases of the business cycle. To do this, tabulate the monthly total deposits series during the 1971–1977 period. This time frame would include the economic expansion of 1971–1973, the severe tight money period of 1973–1974 and the overlapping deep recession of 1973–1975, and the recovery period that began in the spring of 1975. Second, to facilitate analysis, chart the series on arithmetic or semilogarithmic paper. Third, analyze forecasts of economic, financial, and competitive conditions over the planning cycle (usually one year). Some banks also have three and five-year plans; however, over the last decade, most economic and financial forecasts have proven very unreliable. Fourth, taking into account past trends in deposits and expected conditions, forecast the monthly total deposits series.[4] Finally, taking into consideration its attitude toward the risk of having inadequate liquidity, management should make an estimate of the volatile element in average total deposits that it wishes to match with liquid funds. In Figures 2-1 and 2-2, 6.4 percent of total deposits are estimated to be volatile, and 93.6 percent are expected to be reliable.[5]

The task of estimating volatility in the remaining liability and capital accounts is simpler. As with deposits, management estimates the average balance expected over the coming year.

Federal funds purchased are totally volatile, as shown by the failure of the Franklin National Bank. Before this bank failed, there were days when bank borrowing of federal funds exceeded $1 billion or about 25 percent of total liabilities.[6] During its final days, Franklin National was squeezed very hard when a number of banks refused to rollover their federal funds to the beleaguered bank. Perhaps more than any other factor, poor liquidity planning led to the downfall of Franklin National.

"Other liabilities" consist of a variety of accounts. Some items such as short-term liabilities for expenses incurred would be classified as volatile; others, such as the long-term portion of "mortgages payable," would be totally reliable. Each liability must be individually analyzed and classified.

Finally, shareholders' equity is a totally reliable account, since shareholders do not have the right or privilege to demand cash for their shares from the bank.

---

[4]Ideally, banks not only should forecast total deposits, but prepare *pro forma* balance sheets and income statements in conjunction with an overall profit plan.

[5]Kaufman and Lee propose a somewhat more complex technique, which involves fitting a trend line to the total deposit data and constructing confidence limits about the trend line. See Kaufman and Lee, pp. 60–61.

[6]Sanford Rose, "What Really Went Wrong at Franklin National." *Fortune,* October 1974, p. 224.

Figure 2-2. Sample National Bank Summary Report.

ASSETS	LIQUID ASSETS		NON-LIQUID ASSETS		AVERAGE BALANCE
	%	$ (000)	%	$ (000)	$ (000)
Total cash assets	5.0	1,544	95.0	29,522	31,066
Total investments	42.0	30,315	58.0	41,892	72,207
Total loans	-0.5	-825	100.5	157,420	156,595
Total other assets	13.8	1,169	86.2	7,296	8,465
Total assets	12.0	32,203*	88.0	236,130	268,133

LIABILITIES AND CAPITAL	VOLATILE FUNDS		RELIABLE FUNDS		AVERAGE BALANCE
	%	$ (000)	%	$ (000)	$ (000)
Total deposits	6.4	14,063	93.6	205,674	219,737
Total borrowed funds	100.0	17,309	0	0	17,309
Other liabilities	8.8	898	91.2	9,313	10,211
Shareholders' equity	0	0	100.0	21,076	21,076
Total liabilities and equity	12.0	32,270	88.0	236,063	268,333

ANALYSIS	%	$
Total liquid assets	100.0	32,203
Less total volatile funds	100.2	32,270
Excess (deficit) liquidity		(67)
Liquidity ratio (liquid assets: volatile funds)	1.00	

*Net liquid assets.

Source: Article by Daniel J. Kaufman, Jr. and David R. Lee, "Planning Liquidity: A Practical Approach." Bank Administration Institute, *The Magazine of Bank Administration*, February, 1977, p. 58.

Part II: Classify Assets Either as Liquid or Non-liquid. The next task is to measure the bank's ability to meet its liquidity needs from assets. To do this, management must classify assets either as liquid or non-liquid. *Liquid assets* essentially are excess cash assets, plus other assets that can be turned into cash with little or no loss. *Non-liquid assets* are those assets unavailable to meet liquidity needs.

Beginning with cash assets, practically all vault cash, balances at the Fed, cash items in the process of collection, and correspondent balances are required and/or necessary for the conduct of business. Therefore, the great bulk of these assets are illiquid. If deposits decline, some portion of cash assets would shift from required to excess and, hence, become "liquid." The extent to which this occurs would depend on the composition of deposits at the lower level. However, the increasing trend in the ratio of currency-to-demand deposits held by the public may necessitate more vault cash for working reserves, thus negating somewhat (if not totally) the effect of a deposit decline on required reserves. Each bank should consider these factors and all others in its market which bear on the amount of possible liquidity in its cash assets, but generally, only about 5 percent of all cash assets should be considered liquid.

In the investment portfolio, federal funds sold and securities purchased with agreements to resell may be considered liquid. However, the Franklin National Bank case made many bankers aware that federal funds sold may not be totally liquid if the purchasing bank fails. With respect to the remaining investment portfolio, securities pledged against public deposits are illiquid. The remaining securities should be classified as liquid or illiquid, depending upon their ability to be sold with little or no loss in market value. Securities with a maturity of one year or less are considered liquid because changes in market rates of interest upward have little effect on their market value.

Loan liquidity is difficult to evaluate. Most of the time, banks are faced with more legitimate credit demands than they can fill. Moreover, during crisis periods, requests for loan renewals and the volume of defaults and slow payers increase. However, through control of credit extensions, there is some marginal amount of loan liquidity available in the installment loan and mortgage loan portfolios. Both of these loan types generate monthly payments. Also, to the extent that these borrowers pay with checks on other banks, there is an increase in cash assets equal to the loan repayment. After evaluation, perhaps no more than 5 to 10 percent of the installment and mortgage loan portfolio may be considered liquid.

Charge card and overdraft loans should be classified as illiquid, primarily because the level of the former generally will remain stable, while the latter is a risky asset.

The commercial loan portfolio cannot be considered a reliable source of liquidity because of requests for renewals and new credit extensions. At most banks, the demand for commercial loans is highly cyclical and a great potential source of liquidity needs. We can incorporate this need for liquidity to meet future commercial loan demand by expressing it as a negative number in the liquid assets column, as in Figure 2-1. Management should estimate the highest level that commercial loans might rise above the expected average level for the coming year and the highest level that management is willing to let it rise given the expected structure of assets and liabilities. The difference between the lowest of these two estimates and expected average level expressed as a negative percentage of the expected average should be entered under the liquid asset column for commercial loans.

Premises and equipment obviously are illiquid. Other assets should be examined and classified individually.

Part III: Compare the Volume of Liquid Assets with the Volume of Volatile Funds. Figure 2-2 contains a summary liquidity report developed from data in Figure 2-1. Liquid assets total $32,203,000, as compared with $32,270,000 in volatile funds, thus producing a liquidity deficit of $67,000 and a liquid ratio (liquid assets to volatile funds) of 1.00. This is a "balanced liquidity position"; i.e., the estimated potential demand for liquidity is balanced with bank holdings of liquid assets.

An Evaluation

For management, the liquidity planning and analysis system proposed here should be helpful for several reasons: it provides a framework for estimating the bank's liquidity needs and its ability to meet these needs; it permits management to express its risk preferences with respect to potential deposit volatility; and finally, this system clearly shows bankers that every asset and liability management decision has an impact not only on profits, but on liquidity as well.

The system outlined here would be considered too conservative by money market banks because it calls for the bank to hold net liquid assets equal to volatile funds. Money market banks with access to nation-wide and world-wide sources of funds rely extensively on a wide range of liability management techniques. In addition, they tend to view liquidity management in more of a short-run framework than do small and medium-sized banks. This is because with a good reputation and at a price, they can buy their liquidity needs on a daily basis. Also, if the cost of funds rises, money market banks are in a better position to pass along much of these cost increases, because the yield on at least 75 percent of their commercial loans is tied to the prime rate, which tends to escalate during tight money periods.[7]

The system proposed here, in more elaborate form, may be used by money market banks. These institutions have annual or three-to-five-year profit plans that entail balance sheet forecasts. However, instead of adopting a ratio of liquid assets to volatile funds of 1.0, management could adopt a lower ratio of, say, 0.5 and plan to cover unusual needs for liquidity through liability management techniques. This exchange of liquid for illiquid assets does tend to increase profitability, which enhances the bank's reputation and ability to buy funds with liability management techniques; but it must be recognized that if all money market banks are counting on meeting their liquidity needs in this matter, there may be times, such as the 1973–1974 credit crunch, when the cost of raising funds has a severe impact on profits.

TECHNIQUES OF LIQUIDITY ANALYSIS FOR "OUTSIDERS"

Data Available

Those without access to internal bank records must use published statements of condition and quarterly and annual reports as their primary sources of data for evaluating bank liquidity. A bank's latest annual report is the best source because it contains comparative statements of condition, usually over a five-year period and these statements are adjusted to reflect developments such as mergers and changes in accounting principles. The annual report usually includes maturity schedules for investment securities, CD's,

---

[7]An excellent discussion of the dimensions of liquidity management at a money market bank is contained in the 1976 Citicorp *Annual Report,* pp. 24–27.

and other borrowed money. Data on individual banks should be compared with those of banks of similar asset size or deposit composition. These data are available in the FDIC's quarterly report of assets and liabilities of insured commercial banks and in the *Federal Reserve Bulletin.*

Liquidity Ratios

Liquidity ratios provide the primary means of judging a bank's liquidity position. For business firms, credit analysts for years have used the "current ratio" (current assets divided by current liabilities) and the "acid test ratio" (current assets minus inventory divided by current liabilities) to measure a firm's liquidity. Typically, a firm with a current ratio of 2:1 is adjudged liquid. However, for banks there are no universally recognized liquidity ratios. One reason for this is that liabilities of non-financial firms are highly predictable because they have fixed maturities, while a large percentage of bank liabilities are due on demand. Because there is no firm agreement on which bank liquidity ratios are best, a number of ratios will be presented and evaluated here.

$$\frac{\text{Cash Assets}}{\text{Total Deposits}} \qquad (1)$$

In this ratio (1), cash assets include currency and coin, reserves with the Federal Reserve, balances with banks in the U.S. and foreign countries, and cash items in the process of collection. Sometimes this is "the" ratio advanced as a measure of bank liquidity; however, as pointed out earlier, most cash assets are unavailable to meet liquidity needs, and total deposits is not a perfect measure of liquidity needs. Trends in this ratio are shown in Table 2-1.

Two conclusions are apparent from the data shown: (1) above the $10 million mark in assets, the amount of cash assets held increases with size; and (2) the ratio has declined since 1970, especially for banks with assets of $1 billion and below. The ratio of cash to deposits increases with size for three reasons: (1) reserve ratios increase with deposit size; (2) cash items in the process of collection increase with size because of the check volume among large account

Table 2-1. Ratio of Cash Assets to Total Deposits, by Size of Insured Bank, 1970–1977

December 31	All Banks	Banks with Assets of: 10 million or less	10–25 million	25–100 million	100–500 million	500 million – 1 billion	1 billion or more
1970	19.4	14.3	13.3	14.4	18.7	19.9	24.9
1971	18.5	13.0	12.7	13.5	17.3	18.8	24.1
1972	18.3	12.9	12.0	12.6	17.0	17.3	24.4
1973	17.3	12.7	11.9	12.6	16.4	16.7	22.2
1974	17.1	12.8	11.6	12.7	16.8	17.3	20.9
1975	17.0	12.0	11.3	12.1	16.0	17.2	21.7
1976	15.7	11.4	10.5	10.7	13.3	15.4	20.5
1977	17.3	11.2	10.5	10.9	13.6	17.1	23.3

Source: Calculated from FDIC, *Assets and Liabilities of Insured Commercial Banks,* annual; and unpublished data.

Note: Cash assets include currency and coin, reserves with the Federal Reserve, balances with banks in the U.S. and foreign countries, and cash items in the process of collection.

holders; and larger banks hold higher balances in foreign banks. The trend downward in the cash to deposits ratio since 1970 reflects a slight decrease in the reserve ratios, but primarily reflects bank efforts to economize on cash assets holdings and improved check collection procedures by banks and the Fed. In conclusion, the cash assets to deposits ratio is an imperfect measure of an individual bank's liquidity but is nevertheless a ratio that should be examined.

$$\frac{\text{Securities} + \text{Net Federal Funds Sold}}{\text{Total Deposits}} \qquad (2)$$

"Securities" include all obligations of the U.S. Treasury, agencies, municipals, other securities, and trading account securities; "net federal funds" sold equals federal funds sold and securities purchased under agreements to resell, minus fed funds purchased plus securities sold under agreements to repurchase. Although it is recognized that long-term securities, especially municipals, are somewhat illiquid, most small and medium sized banks consider their securities portfolios their primary sources of liquidity. Some portion of this portfolio could be liquidated with little or no loss. Federal funds sold, of course, is a "near cash" asset.

Table 2-2 contains some significant information. First, this ratio is inversely related to the size of the bank. This is primarily

Table 2-2.   Ratio of Securities + Net Federal Funds Sold to Total Deposits, by Size of Insured Bank, 1970-1977.

December 31	All Banks	Banks with Assets of:					
		10 million or less	10-25 million	25-100 million	100-500 million	500 million- 1 billion	1 billion or more
1970	30.6	43.6	41.3	38.2	31.5	27.2	21.5
1971	30.7	44.8	42.7	40.3	33.0	28.5	19.9
1972	28.7	45.2	42.0	39.1	32.1	27.4	16.6
1973	25.4	45.7	41.2	35.8	29.0	24.2	12.4
1974	24.4	45.0	39.8	35.7	27.9	22.6	12.6
1975	27.4	43.7	41.6	37.5	32.0	27.0	18.2
1976	27.2	40.7	39.5	38.1	34.3	29.0	15.3
1977	27.9	38.5	37.2	35.4	32.0	26.0	12.7

Source: Calculated from FDIC, *Assets and Liabilities of Insured Commercial Banks,* annual; and unpublished data.

Note: "Securities" include all U.S. Treasury, agency, municipal, and other obligations, plus trading account securities. "Net federal funds sold" equals federal funds sold and securities purchased under agreements to resell, minus federal funds purchased, plus securities sold under agreements to repurchase.

because banks above $300 million in assets tend to be net buyers of federal funds and hold relatively smaller securities positions. This ratio might be a good indication of the extent to which larger banks   depend   on   liability   management   techniques   for   liquidity purposes.   This dependency also was demonstrated clearly during the 1973-1974 tight money period when this ratio for banks with assets of $1 billion or more fell to an average of only 12.5 percent.   It rebounded sharply in 1975 as loan demand fell and overall money and credit conditions improved.   This ratio, along with others, is helpful in evaluating a bank's liquidity position.

$$\frac{\begin{array}{l}\text{U.S. Treasury Securities + Agency Obligations}\\\text{+ Net Federal Funds Sold − Other Liabilities}\\\text{for Borrowed Money}\end{array}}{\text{Total Assets}} \qquad (3)$$

The objective of this ratio (3) is to measure the net liquidity of a bank's total asset portfolio after making deductions for federal funds purchased and securities sold under agreement to repurchase and other liabilities for borrowed money. The presumption underlying this ratio is that Treasury and agency securities and federal funds sold are the most liquid assets held by banks. Banks can meet liquidity needs quickly from their holdings of these assets. However, a portion of these securities are pledged against Treasury and other public deposits. Therefore, analysts may want to reduce the numerator by an estimate of the average deposits held for the U.S. Treasury. At most banks, municipals are the primary security pledged against deposits of states and political subdivisions.

Trends in this ratio are shown in Table 2-3. Again, this measure of liquidity varies inversely with bank size. The data show the decline in liquidity during the 1973–1974 tight money period, when banks reduced their holdings of these assets to meet credit demands and deposit drains. These ratios rebounded in 1975 as money and credit conditions improved and interest rates abated.

$$\frac{\text{Federal Funds Purchased and Securities Sold Under Agreement to Repurchase + Other Liabilities for Borrowed Money}}{\text{Total Assets}} \qquad (4)$$

The objective of this ratio (4) is to measure the extent to which a bank's assets are financed with short-term funds. From a traditional viewpoint, the higher this ratio, the less liquid the bank. As can be

Table 2-3. Ratio of U.S. Treasury Securities + Agency Obligation + Net Federal Funds Sold - Other Liabilities for Borrowed Money, to Total Assets, by Size of Insured Bank, 1970-1977.

December 31	All Banks	Banks with Assets of:					
		10 million or less	10–25 million	25–100 million	100–500 million	500 million– 1 billion	1 billion or more
1970	11.9	34.8	22.7	18.5	12.3	8.3	3.9
1971	11.5	28.7	23.3	18.8	12.4	8.3	3.0
1972	10.1	29.0	23.3	18.6	12.4	8.2	0.4
1973	7.1	29.2	21.7	15.6	10.2	6.0	-3.2
1974	7.1	26.5	20.0	15.3	8.8	4.8	-0.7
1975	9.7	26.6	21.1	17.0	12.3	7.8	1.9
1976	10.1	27.6	22.8	19.5	16.1	10.9	1.0
1977	8.1	26.7	21.7	17.6	14.4	8.6	-0.6

Source: Calculated from FDIC, *Assets and Liabilities of Insured Commercial Banks*, annual; and unpublished data.

Note: U.S. Treasury securities and agency obligations held in the trading account are excluded.

Table 2-4. Ratio of Federal Funds Purchased and Securities Sold Under Agreements to Repurchase + Other Liabilities for Borrowed Money to Total Assets, by Size of Bank, 1970-1977.

| December 31 | All Banks | Banks with Assets of: | | | | | |
		10 million or less	10-25 million	25-100 million	100-500 million	500 million-1 billion	1 billion or more
1970	3.0	0.2	0.2	0.8	2.5	5.1	5.8
1971	4.0	0.2	0.3	0.8	3.1	5.3	7.1
1972	5.2	0.3	0.3	1.0	3.7	5.8	9.1
1973	7.0	0.4	0.6	1.6	5.1	7.4	12.2
1974	6.3	0.9	0.8	1.7	5.6	8.2	9.7
1975	6.2	0.7	1.0	1.3	5.3	7.2	10.0
1976	7.5	0.4	0.5	1.1	3.8	7.9	13.3
1977	7.9	0.3	0.5	1.1	3.8	8.8	13.2

Source: Calculated from FDIC, *Assets and Liabilities of Insured Commercial Banks,* annual; and unpublished data.

seen in Table 2-4, this ratio varies directly with the size of the bank. Money market banks, especially, use federal funds to finance longer-term assets such as loans. When money and credit conditions are easy, this usually is a profitable position; however, the danger comes when conditions tighten. As mentioned earlier, the use of federal funds to finance a large percentage of assets was instrumental in the downfall of Franklin National Bank. Therefore, an above average level of this ratio should be a caution signal to anyone attempting to evaluate a bank's liquidity.

$$\frac{\text{Loans}}{\text{Deposits}} \qquad (5)$$

The loans to deposits ratio is the most venerable and frequently cited ratio in banking. To those using this ratio, it is a measure of bank liquidity; the higher the ratio, the lower the liquidity. This is true, but only under some very important assumptions. Like all liquidity ratios that can be developed by outsiders, it indicates nothing about future loan demands or expected deposit withdrawals. Also, it indicates nothing about the liquidity of the remaining assets or the nature of a bank's other liabilities, which, as we have seen, could be a source of great liquidity need.

Table 2-5.   Ratio of Loans to Deposits, by Size of Bank, 1970-1977.

December 31	All Banks	Banks with Assets of:					
		10 million or less	10-25 million	25-100 million	100-500 million	500 million-1 billion	1 billion or more
1970	60.7	52.8	54.0	56.8	59.2	62.6	66.3
1971	59.8	52.4	53.4	56.2	58.2	61.5	64.8
1972	62.0	52.3	54.4	57.4	59.2	63.4	68.6
1973	66.4	52.9	56.2	60.1	63.2	67.5	74.8
1974	67.0	55.2	57.7	60.4	65.0	67.7	74.1
1975	63.4	56.3	56.7	59.0	61.2	63.4	69.0
1976	63.1	56.9	57.5	58.1	58.8	61.9	69.0
1977	65.1	60.4	61.2	62.2	62.1	64.4	68.8

Source: Calculated from FDIC, *Assets and Liabilities of Insured Commercial Banks,* annual; and unpublished data.

Note: Loans are gross loans less reserve for possible loan losses. Data for 1970-1975 are for all banks, while data for 1975-1977 are for insured banks. Noninsured banks account for less than 3 percent of all banking assets.

Trends in the loans to deposits ratio are shown in Table 2-5. This ratio tends to vary directly with bank size. For all banks, it rose in the 1973-1974 period and fell afterwards.

In spite of the aforementioned criticism, the loans to deposits ratio is useful as one of a group of liquidity ratios; but when it is used alone, it can be a misleading indicator. During the 1973-1974 period, this ratio exceeded 90 percent for several large banks. For these and other banks, an above average loans to deposits ratio is an indication to examine other liquidity ratios.

$$\frac{\text{Loans}}{\text{Assets}} \qquad\qquad (6)$$

The loans to assets ratio (6) is very similar ratio to the loans to deposits ratio and the same comments and criticisms are applicable. (See Table 2-6.) However, Korobow, Stuhr, and Martin indicate that the loans to assets ratio provides one of the six early warning signs of changes in bank financial condition.[9]   Other things equal, a rise in this ratio would indicate lower liquidity and the need to evaluate other liquidity ratios.

[9]Leon Korobow, David P. Stuhr, and Daniel Martin, "A Probabilistic Approach to Early Warning of Changes in Bank Financial Condition,"   Federal Reserve Bank of New York, *Monthly Review,* July, 1976, p. 190.

Table 2-6. Ratio of Total Loans to Total Assets, by Size of Bank, 1970–1977.

December 31	All Banks	Banks with Assets of:					
		10 million or less	10–25 million	25–100 million	100–500 million	500 million– 1 billion	1 billion or more
1970	50.6	46.4	48.1	49.6	50.7	52.0	52.1
1971	50.2	46.3	47.5	49.2	49.8	51.4	51.8
1972	51.7	46.1	48.4	50.2	50.7	52.9	53.8
1973	54.2	46.0	49.7	52.6	53.1	55.0	56.9
1974	54.5	47.1	50.8	52.3	53.6	54.5	57.1
1975	51.7	48.2	49.7	51.3	50.8	51.5	53.0
1976	51.9	50.8	52.1	52.2	51.4	51.4	52.0
1977	53.2	54.0	55.4	56.0	54.4	53.2	51.4

Source: Calculated from FDIC, *Assets and Liabilities of Insured Commercial Banks,* annual; and unpublished data.

Note: Loans are gross loans less reserve for possible loan losses. Data for 1970–1975 are for all banks, while data for 1975–1977 are for insured banks.

$$\frac{\text{Securities With a Maturity of Less Than One year}}{\text{Securities}} \qquad (7)$$

This ratio (7) provides a good indication of the degree of liquidity in the investment portfolio. However, it could be an overstatement of liquidity without knowledge of the amount of these short-term securities pledged for public deposits.

$$\frac{\text{Market Value of Securities}}{\text{Statement Value of Securities}} \qquad (8)$$

This ratio (8) is developed from the notes to a bank's financial statements in the annual report. It indicates the extent to which securities have fallen or risen in value relative to the statement value, which is cost plus or minus accrued discount or premium. In tight money periods, as interest rates rise, market values fall, and the amount of the decline is a direct function of maturity. Those banks that attempt to increase yields by extending maturities generally experience the largest decline in market values when market yields rise. The huge fall in market values during the 1973–1974 period made this ratio a more relevant measure of liquidity. Another reason why market values would tend to fall below statement values is that values fall to reflect greater credit risk, as in the case of New York City obligations. Thus, it is necessary to review closely the notes to a bank's financial statement to determine the extent to which this factor might account for some of the deviation in market value from statement value.

CONCLUDING OBSERVATIONS

There is no precise way to measure a bank's liquidity needs. With access to internal data, management should be better able to evaluate future needs than would outsiders, who must rely on various ratios applied to balance sheet aggregates at different points in time. In this section, we examined a number of these liquidity ratios. The basic aim of most of these ratios is to measure the amount of a bank's liquid assets in relation to total deposits or total assets. When applied to banks of different size, larger banks have much more flexibility in liquidity planning because they can practice liability management techniques in nation-wide and world-wide money markets. Because of this ability, their liquidity planning horizon is much shorter than it is for small banks.

A logical question is: How do we measure a large bank's ability to raise funds through liability management techniques? Liquidity ratios alone do not provide the answer. Successful use of liability management techniques depends on many factors: capital adequacy, past and expected profitability, absolute size, growth rate in deposits and assets, the bank's record in the area of loan losses during the 1973–1975 period, and the general reputation of the bank and its management.

In sum, outsiders who examine liquidity ratios for any bank should look for deviations from industry averages. These deviations are caution signals that the bank's ability to survive in adverse economic conditions has been reduced.

3
Analysis of Bank Capital

In recent years, with the increase in bank failures, analysis of bank capital has received greater attention from banking regulatory authorities, depositors, shareholders, and other bank creditors. This is because capital, in both absolute and relative terms, is a primary indication of a bank's "financial strength" and ability to remain a solvent and viable institution.

In this chapter, we shall (1) examine briefly the forms of bank capital, (2) discuss the functions of bank capital, (3) consider the measurement of capital adequacy, and (4) develop and analyze several important ratios that may be used to analyze capital adequacy.

FORMS OF BANK CAPITAL

Common Stock, Surplus, and Undivided Profits

Capital accounts of most banks consist of common stock (sometimes called capital stock), surplus, and undivided profits. The sum in the *common stock* account is equal to the number of common shares outstanding times the par value of stock. The *surplus* account reflects the sale of common stock at a premium over the par value and accrued profits that have been transferred from the undivided profits account. The *undivided profits* account represents accrued profits and is similar to a non-bank business' earned surplus account. Since few banks have preferred stock outstanding, the sum of common stock, surplus, and undivided profits usually comprises a bank's *equity capital* or the owners' equity in the bank's assets.

Preferred Stock

Preferred stock is a rarely used form of equity capital that gives the owner the right to receive a stated dividend. Preferred stock may be *cummulative,* which means that if the dividend is omitted, past due dividends must be paid on preferred stock before common shareholders can receive dividends. Preferred stock also may be *convertible* or *non-convertible* into shares of the bank's common stock.

The principal advantage of preferred stock over alternative means of raising capital is that the former has no maturity and carries no voting privilege. On the other hand, preferred stock dividends are non-deductible for income tax purposes, which makes the cost of capital from this source very high. Moreover, most investors find preferred stock unattractive since the appreciation potential is limited.

Capital Notes and Debentures

Capital notes and debentures, or subordinated debt or senior debt, as these issues sometimes are called, are long-term obligations to repay money in the future. They carry fixed interest rates, and their claim for repayment is subordinated to that of depositors and other creditors.

Capital notes and debentures may contribute in several ways to improved capital adequacy. First, because their claim is subordinated, capital notes and debentures directly increase a bank's ability to absorb losses in the event of failure. Second, the issuance of capital notes and debentures has a leverage effect, which may lead to an increase in earnings and perhaps dividends.[1] To the extent profits are increased, capital adequacy is enhanced. An improved rate of growth in earnings generally leads to a higher price-earnings ratio, which facilitates the acqustion of additional equity capital.

[1] *Bank financial leverage* is the use of non-shareholder funds such as capital notes and debentures, time and saving deposits, demand deposits, and federal funds purchased in order to increase earnings on shareholders' equity.

As an alternative source of funds, subordinated debt possesses several advantages over time deposits. Banks do not have to hold reserves or pay deposit insurance on subordinated debt, as they do with time deposits. In addition, the administrative costs associated with debt instruments are less than those of time deposits.

As an alternative source of capital, capital notes and debentures offer several advantages over equity capital. First, the interest cost of debt is tax deductible, while dividends on equity capital are not; equity dividends must be paid from after-tax earnings. This tends to make the cost of debt much less than the cost of internally generated funds (undivided profits) as a source of capital.[2] Second, the issuance of debt does not cause a short-run dilution of earnings per share as does the sale of common equity shares. A number of banks have attempted to get the "best of both worlds" by issuing convertible debentures. In the short-run, the bank realizes the advantages of debt, and at a later time, presumably when earnings are greater, it acquires equity capital through conversion.

Subordinated debt did not become a viable source of capital until the Comptroller of the Currency, James J. Saxon, published a ruling in late 1962 permitting national banks to issue these instruments. At the close of 1962, insured banks had only $20.5 million in subordinated debt outstanding. However, by the close of 1977, the total amount had risen to $5.7 billion or 6.7 percent of total equity and debt capital. In the foreseeable future, it is very likely that debt will continue to increase in relative importance as a source of bank capital, since most bank stocks presently are selling below book value per share. In other words, the sale of additional common shares at prices below book value per share would cause dilution for current shareholders. Convertible notes and debentures may offer many banks a viable alternative to the problem caused by low bank stock prices.

---

[2] The cost of internally generated capital can be estimated by the formula $k = D/P + g$, where D is expected dividends, P is current price, and g is the expected appreciation in the stock price. For example, if the expected dividend is $1, the current price is $25, and the expected appreciation rate is 6 percent, then the cost of equity funds is 10 percent (0.04 + 0.06). Investors would not hold the bank's stock if alternative investments with similar risks yielded more than 10 percent.

Reserves for Contingencies and Other Capital Reserves

Also included in bank capital are *reserves for contingencies* and *other capital reserves,* which are funds set aside from undivided profits. An example of a contingency reserve is a reserve established because of a pending lawsuit. Examples of capital reserves are amounts set aside for dividends or for possible retirement of preferred stock. Amounts placed in any of these reserve accounts are non-deductible for income tax purposes.

FUNCTIONS OF BANK CAPITAL

Bank capital serves four functions: (1) it demonstrates ability to absorb unanticipated losses; (2) it provides operating funds; (3) it measures ownership; and (4) it facilitates shareholder pressure toward managerial efficiency.

How Bank Capital Demonstrates Ability to Absorb Unanticipated Losses

The primary function of bank capital is to demonstrate to the public and to the banking authorities the bank's ability to absorb losses.[3] When a loan or investment goes into default, the bank must remove the loan or investment from the asset side of its statement of condition and, in the case of a loan, reduce the "reserve for loan losses." For security losses, the "undivided profits" account or the "reserve for security losses" must be reduced. If losses are large enough to wipe out reserves and undivided profits, the bank is in danger of becoming insolvent; that is, non-owner claims soon may exceed assets. If this happens, banking regulations stipulate that the bank must be closed. Thus, capital and reserves protect depositors and other bank claimholders by serving as cushions for absorbing losses in asset accounts.

Banks expect to suffer some losses in their loan portfolio. Relatively small losses are absorbed out of current earnings since that is the primary source of additions to the "reserve for possible loan losses" account. However, the reserve account usually is not large enough to absorb the *unanticipated* losses on loans and investments that might

[3]Roland I. Robinson and Richard H. Pettway, *Policies for Optimum Bank Capital.* Chicago: Association of Reserve City Bankers, 1967, Chapter 3.

result from severe business fluctuations, inept public policy, local or industry recession, war, or managerial lapses.[4] Bank capital serves as a financial shield to lessen the possibility that uninsured depositors and other claim holders might lose funds if the bank is closed and liquidated.

As a protective cushion, bank capital also has important psychological value. If depositors and borrowers believe that a bank has adequate capital to weather economic storms, the former are less likely to initiate a bank run on deposits, and the latter may be more inclined to pay their obligations on time. The amount of capital a bank has relative to its assets and deposits is an outward demonstration of strength and thereby helps to mitigate the adverse impact that external events might have on the bank. Because of this psychological factor, it seems more accurate to state that the primary function of bank capital is to demonstrate ability to absorb unanticipated losses rather than simply to protect depositors.

How Bank Capital Provides Operating Funds

A prerequisite for a bank's opening for business is that it have adequate quarters. Therefore, for most banks, the first use of funds raised through the issuance of common stock is to purchase fixed assets. Also, as we noted earlier, funds raised through the sale of capital notes and debentures may be used to expand loans and investments.

How Bank Capital Measures Ownership

A function of equity capital in any business is to reflect ownership claims, rather than creditor claims, on assets. At the end of 1977, bank shareholders had claims on only 7.0 percent of the assets of insured commercial banks.

How Bank Capital Facilitates Shareholder Pressure Toward Managerial Efficiency[5]

This is perhaps an overlooked function of bank capital. Unlike all credit unions, mutual savings banks, non-insured private pension

[4]*Ibid.*, pp. 18-19.

[5]George R. Morrison and Richard T. Selden, *Time Deposit Growth and the Employment of Bank Funds.* Chicago: Association of Reserve City Bankers, 1965, p. 66.

funds, and some savings and loan associations and life insurance companies, all banks have shareholders.   Because these investor-owners have a vested interest in bank profitability, it might be that of all classes of financial institutions, banks are under the greatest pressure to operate efficiently.

CAPITAL ADEQUACY

If the primary function of bank capital is to demonstrate ability to absorb unanticipated losses, the logical question is: How much capital is adequate to perform this function?   Banking authorities have wrestled with this problem virtually since the time when banks were first chartered in this country.   In recognition of the need to protect depositors and create a stable banking system, federal and state governments have enacted legal capital requirements to ensure capital adequacy for newly chartered banks.

Legal Requirements

National banking laws provide that no national banking association shall be organized with less than $100,000 in capital, except in places with a population of 6,000 or less, where minimum capital may be $50,000.   In cities with a population of 50,000 or more, the minimum capital is $200,000.   In the outlying districts of a city where the state laws permit organization of state banks with capital of $100,000 or less, national banks may be organized with capital of not less than $100,000.   In addition to these requirements, national banks must begin business with a paid-in-surplus of 20 percent of its capital stock to cover organizational expenses and any initial operating losses.[6]   Many state banking statutes also relate minimum capital to population and have a stipulation that banks begin operation with a minimum amount of capital surplus.   Moreover, in order to establish out-of-town branches, national banks and most state banks must satisfy the same minimum capital stock and surplus requirements that would apply if a new unit bank were going to open in the proposed branch office city.

[6]This 20 percent capital surplus requirement was added in 1933.

It should be apparent that population is not a satisfactory criterion by which to measure capital adequacy. Today, even though the minimum capital requirements still are law, the determination of capital adequacy has become a matter of administrative judgment. However, the decisions of the banking supervisory authorities about capital adequacy are based on legal considerations. Under various statutes, appropriate banking authorities must consider capital adequacy in decisions that involve bank chartering, branching, mergers, and holding company activities. Capital adequacy determination is an important part of every bank examination.

Measurement by Banking Authorities

Neither the Comptroller of the Currency, the FDIC, or the Board of Governors of the Federal Reserve System rely exclusively on such ratios as capital to assets, capital to risk assets (total assets less cash and U.S. Treasury securities), or capital to deposits in their assessment of capital adequacy for the banks they supervise and examine. Rather, each agency considers a number of factors, many of which are non-quantifiable. The Comptroller's position is that national banks are not required to build capital to the point "to be able to absorb the strain of total economic collapse."[7] Rather, examiners "should determine if the level of capital is adequate to permit the bank to operate as a viable institution, capable of responsibly moving funds and providing related services while protecting against unanticipated adversity."[8]

In the determination of capital adequacy, the Comptroller instructs its examiners to consider the following factors:

1. Quality of management
2. Liquidity
3. Asset quality
4. History of earnings and their retention
5. Quality and character of ownership
6. Deposit structure
7. Quality of operating procedures
8. Capacity to meet present and future financial needs.

[7]*Comptroller's Handbook for National Bank Examiners,* Section 303.1, p. 2.
[8]*Ibid.*

CAPITAL RATIOS

Capital ratios represent the primary technique of analyzing capital adequacy. As with liquidity adequacy, true adequacy of capital is determined only after the fact. Deviations of capital ratios for individual banks from national averages provide a good warning signal to both management and outsiders that a closer analysis of capital adequacy is required. Four capital ratios are described below.

Primary Ratios

$$\frac{\text{Equity Capital}}{\text{Total Assets}} \quad\quad (1)$$

The ratio of equity capital to total assets (1) indicates the percentage decline in total assets that could be covered with equity capital. At first glance, this ratio has merit because all assets involve a chance of loss, and any loss or decline in value involves a decrease in a reserve account or shareholders' equity. Therefore, this ratio is a useful measure of capital adequacy.

As may be seen in Table 3-1, the ratio of equity capital to total assets is inversely related to the size of the bank. This reflects the more conservative stance of small banks and the ability of larger banks to reduce their need for capital because they are able to reduce

Table 3-1. Equity Capital to Total Assets, by Size of Bank, 1970-1977.

December 31	All Banks	Banks with Assets of:					
		10 million or less	10–25 million	25–100 million	100–500 million	500 million– 1 billion	1 billion and over
1970	7.5	9.0	7.6	7.6	7.5	7.4	7.1
1971	7.4	9.0	7.5	7.2	7.2	7.3	7.3
1972	7.1	9.0	7.4	7.1	6.9	7.1	6.9
1973	7.0	9.4	7.5	7.2	6.8	7.0	6.5
1974	6.9	9.9	7.7	7.4	7.0	7.0	6.2
1975	7.2	10.1	7.8	7.5	7.0	7.0	6.8
1976	7.2	9.7	8.1	7.6	7.1	6.7	6.8
1977	7.0	9.6	8.1	7.6	6.9	6.5	6.6

Source: FDIC, *Report of Income: Commercial and Mutual Savings Banks,* annual.

Note: Data for 1970-1975 are for all commercial banks; data for 1976-1977 are for insured commercial banks.

Table 3-2. Risk Asset Ratio = Equity Capital to (Total Assets – Cash – U.S. Treasury Securities), by Size of Bank, 1970–1977.

December 31	All Banks	Banks with Assets of:					
		10 million or less	10–25 million	25–100 million	100–500 million	500 million– 1 billion	1 billion and over
1970	10.1	13.2	10.5	10.1	10.0	9.9	9.7
1971	9.9	12.8	10.1	9.4	9.5	9.6	9.8
1972	9.4	12.6	9.7	9.0	9.0	9.2	9.2
1973	8.8	12.4	9.6	8.9	8.6	8.7	8.3
1974	8.6	12.8	9.6	9.2	8.6	8.7	7.8
1975	9.3	13.2	9.8	9.4	8.9	9.0	8.9
1976	9.3	12.6	10.3	9.6	9.1	8.6	8.9
1977	9.0	12.6	10.2	9.4	8.8	8.5	8.7

Source: FDIC, *Report of Income: Commercial and Mutual Savings Banks,* annual.

Note: Data for 1970–1975 are for all commercial banks; data for 1976–1977 are for insured commercial banks.

the adverse effects of the default risk and the market risk through the law of large numbers. Thus far in the 1970's, the capital to total assets ratio has increased slightly for banks under $25 million and declined slightly for banks above $100 million.

$$\text{Risk Asset Ratio} = \frac{\text{Equity Capital}}{\text{Total Assets} - \text{Cash} - \text{U.S. Treasury Securities}} \quad (2)$$

A principal weakness in the equity capital to total assets ratio is that it does not take into account that some assets, namely cash and short-term U.S. Treasury securities, involve no default or market risk. Because of this weakness, the "risk asset" ratio (2) was developed. This ratio is the same as ratio (1) with the exception that cash and all U.S. Treasury securities are subtracted from total assets in the denominator.[9]

For all bank sizes, the "risk asset" ratio is higher than the equity capital to total assets ratio, and it also varies inversely with size of the bank. As seen in Table 3-2, since 1970, the "risk asset" ratio has drifted downward slightly for all banks especially those with assets of $100 million or more.

[9]The market risk involved with longer term Treasuries is ignored here.

Table 3-3. Secondary Risk Asset Ratio = Equity Capital to (Total Assets - Cash - U.S. Treasury Securities - Agency Obligations - Federal Funds Sold), by Size of Bank, 1970-1977.

December 31	All Banks	Banks with Assets of:					
		10 million or less	10-25 million	25-100 million	100-500 million	500 million- 1 billion	1 billion and over
1970	10.9	15.1	11.7	11.1	10.8	10.6	10.1
1971	10.7	15.1	10.7	10.4	10.3	10.3	10.3
1972	10.2	15.2	11.2	10.2	9.9	9.9	9.7
1973	9.7	15.8	11.2	10.0	9.7	9.6	8.8
1974	9.5	16.1	11.3	10.4	9.7	9.6	8.3
1975	10.3	16.1	11.3	10.5	10.1	10.0	9.6
1976	10.9	15.7	12.0	10.8	10.3	9.8	9.6
1977	10.0	15.3	11.9	10.6	9.8	9.5	9.5

Source: FDIC, *Report of Income: Commercial and Mutual Savings Banks,* annual.

Note: Data for 1970-1975 are for all commercial banks: data for 1976-1977 are for insured commercial banks.

$$\text{Secondary Risk Asset Ratio} = \frac{\text{Equity Capital}}{\text{Total Assets} - \text{Cash} - \text{U.S. Treasury Securities} - \text{Agency Obligations} - \text{Federal Funds Sold}} \quad (3)$$

In recognition of the "low risk" nature of agency obligations and federal funds sold, it is possible to calculate a secondary risk asset ratio (3) by subtracting these items from the denominator of the "risk asset" ratio. As shown in Table 3-3, this increases the ratios for smaller banks because, typically, federal funds sold are an important asset to these banks. This ratio also has declined slightly since 1970.

$$\frac{\text{Equity Capital} + \text{Capital Notes and Debentures} + \text{Reserves for Possible Loan Losses}}{\text{Total Loans}} \quad (4)$$

This capital ratio (4) involves a broader view of capital and has only total loans in the denominator. Inclusion of capital notes and debentures in the numerator is an acknowledgment that since the mid-1960's banking regulatory authorities have permitted senior capital to supplement equity capital for purposes of capital adequacy analysis. Also, since the majority of the risk is in the loan portfolio, total loans is a meaningful risk proxy in the denominator.

Table 3-4. Equity Capital + Capital Notes and Debentures + Reserves for Possible Loan Losses to Total Loans, by Size of Bank, 1970-1977.

December 31	All Banks	Banks with Assets of:					
		10 million or less	10-25 million	25-100 million	100-500 million	500 million-1 billion	1 billion and over
1970	16.4	20.4	17.4	16.7	16.3	15.9	15.7
1971	16.3	20.4	17.0	15.9	15.8	15.6	15.9
1972	15.2	17.7	16.4	15.4	14.9	14.8	14.6
1973	14.3	21.3	16.3	14.8	14.2	14.2	13.1
1974	14.1	22.0	16.5	15.5	14.4	14.4	12.5
1975	15.3	21.8	16.7	15.8	15.0	15.1	14.5
1976	15.6	19.6	16.3	15.6	15.4	15.0	15.5
1977	15.0	18.6	15.7	14.8	14.5	14.2	15.2

Source: FDIC, *Report of Income: Commercial and Mutual Savings Banks,* annual.

Note: Data for 1970-1975 are for all commercial banks; data for 1976-1977 are for insured commercial banks. For 1976 and 1977, data for "gross loans" was used for total loans. The terms are equivalent.

Table 3-4 shows that there is very little difference in this ratio among bank classes above $10 million. This ratio did fall rather significantly in 1974 for banks above $1 billion, but recovered subsequently.

Other Ratios

Variations from the above four ratios may be developed quite easily. Senior debt and the reserve for possible loan losses could be added to equity capital in the first three ratios. Or, in the secondary risk asset ratio, short-term, high-grade municipals could be subtracted from the denominator to reflect the minimum risk nature of these assets.

The capital to deposits ratio was omitted purposefully because, although it has been used for many years by some bankers and regulatory authorities, its value is limited since deposits are not a suitable proxy for risk.

4
The Bank
Income Statement

The *bank income statement* contains a listing of all operating income and expense items, as well as three measures of bank income. The income statement is like a report card; it reveals how well management has done in generating a profit for shareholders. If profits are above or below average, analysis of the income statement itself and income statement items in relation to statement of condition items usually will suggest the probable reason for the departure from average levels. In this chapter, we shall (1) examine the nature of each item on the income statement, (2) explain how to use composition analysis and percentage increase analysis of the income statement to make an initial evaluation of profitability, and (3) describe the three measures of bank income. The income and expense concepts are essential for understanding the analytical techniques developed in Chapters 5–7. For a description of the assets and liabilities that generate the bulk of the income and expense flows, see Chapter 1.

OPERATING INCOME

Assets are the primary source of bank income. However, in recent years, banks have strived to develop sources of income, such as investment underwriting and trust management, that do not involve a utilization of bank assets. Each of the major operating income items on the income statement is examined briefly below.

Table 4-1. Operating Income of Insured Commercial Banks, Selected Years, 1965-1977 (Millions of Dollars).

Year	Total	Interest and Fees on Loans[a]		Interest on Balances with Banks[c]		Income on Federal Funds Sold and Securities Purchased under Resale Agreements[a]		Interest on Treasuries		Interest and Dividends on Agencies[b]		Interest on Municipals[b]	
		Amount	Percent	Amount	Percent	Amount	Percent	Amount	Percent	Amount	Percent	Amount	Percent
1965	16,817	11,205	66.6					2,225	13.2				
1970	34,716	22,967	66.2			1,006	2.9	3,079	8.9	688	2.0	2,620	7.6
1973	53,036	35,376	66.7			2,487	4.7	3,465	6.5	1,472	2.8	3,865	7.3
1974	68,161	47,139	69.2			3,712	5.4	3,441	5.0	2,019	3.0	4,454	6.5
1975	66,559	43,380	65.2			2,295	3.4	4,441	6.7	2,349	3.5	4,919	7.4
1976	80,664	51,645	64.0	4,487	5.6	1,985	2.5	5,976	7.4	2,415	3.0	5,135	6.4
1977	90,069	58,811	65.3	4,860	5.4	2,471	2.7	6,369	7.1	2,466	2.7	5,338	5.9

Year	Interest and Dividends on Other Securities		Income from Direct Lease Financing[c]		Trust Department Income		Service Charges on Deposit Accounts		Other Service Charges, Commissions, and Fees		Other Operating Income	
	Amount	Percent	Amount	Percent	Amount	Percent	Amount	Percent	Amount	Percent	Amount	Percent
1965	1,285	7.6			690	4.1	843	5.0	304	1.8	266	1.6
1970	152	.4			1,132	3.3	1,178	3.4	842	2.4	1,050	3.0
1973	372	.7			1,460	2.8	1,327	2.5	1,262	2.4	1,961	3.7
1974	468	.7			1,502	2.2	1,460	2.1	1,409	2.1	2,554	3.7
1975	533	.8			1,602	2.4	1,555	2.3	1,654	2.5	3,832	5.8
1976	856	1.1	534	0.7	1,795	2.2	1,635	2.0	2,183	2.7	2,018	2.5
1977	967	1.1	699	0.8	1,980	2.2	1,797	2.0	2,404	2.7	1,903	2.1

Source: FDIC, Annual Reports and Federal Reserve Bulletin.
Note: Details may not add due to rounding.
a."Income on federal funds sold and repos" is included in "interest and discounts on loans" for 1968 and prior years.
b."Interest and dividends on agencies" and "interest on municipals" are included in "interest and dividends on securities" for 1968 and prior years.
cFigures not available before 1976.

Interest and Fees on Loans

Interest and fees on loans are the largest income item, accounting for nearly two-thirds of operating income for insured banks (Table 4-1). Included in this total are all interest and discounts, both current and past due, and fees and similar charges on loans. Also under this heading are points charged on mortgage loans, investigation and service charges, renewal and past due charges, commitment fees, and profits or losses resulting from the sale of loans, acceptances, and commercial paper.

Interest and fees on loans at insured banks more than doubled between 1972 and 1977 because of an 82.6 percent increase in outstanding loans and even more important because the general level of interest rates and fees charged were at historically high levels throughout this period.

Interest on Balances with Other Banks

This income item contains interest income on deposits with other domestic and foreign banks. Prior to 1976, interest on balances with other banks was reported as other income. In 1977, interest on balances with other banks totaled $4.9 billion, and was the fourth largest income category. Virtually all of this income is received by banks with assets above $300 million. A significant part of these balances are held in foreign banks as part of reciprocal deposit relationships.

Interest on Federal Funds Sold and on Securities Purchased Under Resale Agreements

The sale of federal funds and securities purchased under resale agreements represent the primary way that most banks utilize excess reserves on a day-to-day basis. The importance of this income item varies inversely with bank size. Large banks tend to be net buyers of federal funds because they have the loan demand that can be funded with this liability management technique. Small banks tend to practice a more conservative approach to balance sheet management; they consider federal funds sold as an important part of their liquidity position, and they generally do not prefer to finance loans with day-to-day renewals of federal funds purchased. In 1977, interest on fed funds sold and repos represented 2.7 percent of insured bank income.

Interest on Treasuries

Treasury securities are held primarily for liquidity purposes. Between 1965 and 1977, income on Treasuries declined from 13.2 percent to 7.1 percent of operating income. This drop is an indication of the extent that banks have squeezed their liquidity positions to accommodate loan demand.

Interest on Agencies

The term "agencies" includes securities of U.S. agencies and federally-sponsored corporations, such as the Federal Land Banks and Government National Mortgage Corporation (Ginny Mae). As with Treasuries, banks hold agencies primarily for liquidity purposes; however agencies tend to yield slightly more than Treasuries of comparable maturity because the market perceives that agencies have a slightly higher credit risk since they are not direct obligations of the U.S. government. In 1977, interest on agencies represented 2.7 percent of operating income.

Interest on Municipals

The term "municipals" includes the obligations of states and their potential subdivisions; cities, counties, school districts, and other public authorities. The principal attraction of these securities is that the interest income is exempt from federal and state income tax in the state of issue. In 1977, income on municipals represented 8.4 percent of operating income for banks under $300 million in assets, but 4.6 percent for banks over $300 million. The primary reason for this is that the larger banks tend to have domestic and international loans that are more profitable than an equivalent amount of municipals.

Interest and Dividends on Other Securities

"Other securities" include investments in unconsolidated subsidiaries and associated companies, the Asian Development Bank, the International Bank for Reconstruction and Development (World Bank), and Federal Reserve stock. In 1977, this income item comprised only 1.1 percent of operating income.

Income from Direct Lease Financing

Income from direct lease financing includes that received from property such as airliners, ships, trucks, and many other forms of equipment. Even though this income item increased by 30.9 percent between 1976 and 1977, it comprised only 0.8 percent of bank operating income in 1977. Banks with assets above $300 million received 91.8 percent of all bank income from direct lease financing.

Income from Fiduciary Activities

Bank income from fiduciary activities nearly tripled between 1965 and 1977, although, as a percentage of operating income, it fell from 4.1 to 2.2 percent. The 424 banks with assets above $300 million earned 83.8 percent of all income from trust activities. Essentially, it is the large banks that hold the pension funds of giant corporations. For example, at the end of 1977, Morgan Guaranty Trust Company had assets of $31.7 billion, and managed trust assets of $25.6 billion. Many smaller banks find that their trust activities are unprofitable.

Service Charges on Deposit Accounts

Typically, banks levy a fixed maintenance fee and various activity fees on the personal and business demand deposit accounts they hold. In recent years, banks in some areas of the country have offered "free checking" accounts if a certain minimum balance, such as $100, is maintained. Although bank service charges do not fully cover the expense of providing demand deposit accounts and deposit transfers, they do offset to some degree the cost incurred. As a percentage of operating income, service charge income declined from 5.0 percent in 1965 to 2.0 percent in 1977. Because of declining profit margins, most banks are re-evaluating very carefully the cost of providing the demand deposit function and many have raised their service charges, either directly, or indirectly, by raising the minimum balance requirement.

Other Service Charges

"Other service charges" includes commissions on the sale of insurance policies and the collection of premiums; charges for collecting checks, notes, and bills of exchange; the collection of bills for public utilities and other firms; the sale of bank drafts; the acceptance of bills of exchange; the purchase and sale of securities, acceptances, and commercial paper for banks and other customers; the negotiation of loans for customers or correspondents; the underwriting and sale of securities as permitted by statute; the lending of securities owned by the bank; the servicing of real estate mortgages or other loans held by others; percentage charges to merchants for handling credit cards or charge sales when the bank does not carry the related loan accounts on its books; data processing services; and reimbursements received for services in redeeming U.S. savings bonds. "Other service charges" increased almost eight-fold between 1965 and 1977, as banks strived to increase income from sources that did not involve the commitment of assets.

Other Income

"Other income" consists of net remittable income from subsidiaries and Edge Act Corporations not consolidated; gross rentals from real estate other than bank premises and safe deposit boxes; net trading account income, net cash overages, recoveries on payment of checks over stop payment orders, and similar recurring operating transactions; and recoveries on securities previously charged off.

OPERATING EXPENSES

Salaries, Wages, Pensions, and Other Benefits

Under this heading are the compensations paid to all full-time officers and employees, and part-time employees other than "office temporaries" and contracted guards, including dining room and cafeteria employees, but excluding salaries and employee benefits of officers and employees who are primarily concerned with banking premises and related functions. Also included are contributions to retirement

Year	Total[a]	Salaries, Wages, Pensions, and Other Benefits		Interest on Time Certificates on Deposit of $100,000 or more[c]		Interest on Deposits in Foreign Offices[d]		Interest on Other Deposits		Expense of Federal Funds Purchased and Securities Sold under Agreements to Repurchase[b]		Interest on Other Borrowed Money	
		Amount	Percent	Amount	Percent	Amount	Percent	Amount	Percent	Amount	Percent	Amount	Percent
1965	12,486	4,288	34.3					5,071	40.6			190	1.5
1970	27,589	7,717	28.0					10,484	38.0	1,401	5.1	465	1.7
1973	44,330	10,128	22.8					19,835	44.7	3,899	8.8	504	1.1
1974	58,910	11,587	19.7					27,888	47.3	5,986	10.2	918	1.6
1975	57,582	12,686	22.0					26,246	45.6	3,323	5.8	377	0.6
1976	70,750	14,752	20.9	7,111	10.1	8,750	12.4	19,143	27.1	3,312	4.7	667	0.9
1977	78,484	16,276	20.7	6,732	8.6	10,216	13.0	21,753	27.7	4,536	5.8	816	1.0

Year	Interest on Capital Notes and Debentures[a]		Net Occupancy Expense		Furniture and Equipment, etc.		Provision for Loan Losses[a]		Other Operating Expenses	
	Amount	Percent	Amount	Percent	Amount	Percent	Amount	Percent	Amount	Percent
1965			732	5.9	412	3.3			1,795	14.4
1970	105	0.4	1,255	4.5	909	3.3	703	2.5	4,551	16.5
1973	254	0.6	1,783	4.0	1,201	2.7	1,265	2.9	5,461	12.3
1974	283	0.5	2,052	3.5	1,361	2.3	2,286	3.9	6,549	11.1
1975	294	0.5	2,325	4.0	1,533	2.7	3,612	6.3	7,185	12.5
1976	344	0.5	2,765	3.9	1,721	2.4	3,691	5.2	8,492	12.0
1977	391	0.5	3,036	3.9	1,923	2.5	3,244	4.1	9,561	12.2

Source: FDIC, *Annual Reports* and *Federal Reserve Bulletin*.

Note: Details may not add due to rounding.

[a]"Interest on capital notes and debentures" and "provision for loan losses" are not included in "operating expense total" for 1968 and prior years.

[b]"Expense of federal funds purchased and securities sold under repurchase agreements" are included in "interest on borrowed money" for 1968 and prior years.

[c]Included in "interest on other deposits" before 1976.

[d]Figures not available before 1976.

or pension plans; life insurance premiums less dividends received; hospitalization insurance premiums; unemployment and social security taxes paid; the net cost of employee dining rooms, restaurants, and cafeterias; the cost of medical or health services; and other fringe benefits provided officers and employees. Pensions and other benefits generally comprise about one-sixth of total compensation.

As a percentage of operating expense, total compensation declined from 34.3 percent in 1965 to 20.7 percent in 1977. (See Table 4-2.) During this period, total compensation increased 279.6 percent, while the number of officers and employees rose 87.7 percent. The improvement in average compensation reflects both improved productivity and cost-of-living adjustments. Productivity gains stem primarily from large investments in labor-saving capital, such as data processing equipment, as well as from staffs that are better-educated and trained. Because banking is a very labor intensive industry with large amounts of paper to process, it seems certain that there are extensive unrealized productivity gains waiting to be tapped with the increasing use of capital and improved technology. As this occurs, and if the cost of living continues to advance, average compensation in the foreseeable future should rise at an above average rate.

Interest on Deposits

Since 1965, one of the most important developments in banking has been the dramatic increase in time and savings deposits as a source of funds. Between 1965 and 1977, time and savings deposits increased from 44.6 percent to 59.2 percent of total domestic deposits. The general level of interest rates also increased sharply after 1965. These two factors in combination boosted interest expense on time and savings as a percentage of operating expense from 40.6 percent in 1965 to 49.3 percent in 1977.

Because of the growing significance of this expense item, in 1976, banking regulatory authorities requested that banks report interest expenses under three headings: (1) interest on CD's over $100,000, (2) interest on deposits in foreign offices, and (3) interest on other deposits. This new breakdown facilitates the analysis of this major expense item. For individual banks, the item "interest expense on CD's over $100,000" and "interest on deposits in foreign offices" are important individual expense categories because they measure the cost of raising funds through two very interest-sensitive sources. In 1977, "interest expense on CD's over $100,000" accounted for 8.6 percent of operating expenses, while "interest on deposits in foreign offices" represented 13.0 percent of operating expenses. Virtually all of the latter expense was incurred by banks with assets above $300 million. "Interest on other deposits" represents the expense incurred for smaller CD's and the various savings plans offered.

Expenses of Federal Funds Purchased and Securities Sold Under Agreement to Repurchase in Domestic Offices

This expense item is essentially a "big bank" phenomenon; 93.0 percent of the total incurred in 1977 was by banks with assets over $300 million. As pointed out previously, for these banks, federal funds purchased and securities sold under repo agreements is an important source of funds and one of the primary liability management techniques.

Interest on Other Borrowed Money

"Interest on other borrowed money" includes the interest expense and discount on bills payable, promissory notes, rediscounts, participation sales in pools of loans, borrowings from the Fed, and other short-term instruments issued for the purpose of borrowing money. Again, the sources of funds generating this expense are used primarily by the banks with assets above $300 million; in 1977, this expense item at these banks accounted for 95.4 percent of the total for insured banks.

Interest on Subordinated Notes and Debentures

Subordinated notes and debentures are increasing in importance as a form of capital to augment equity capital. However, as an expense item, it still represents only 0.5 percent of total operating expense.

Net Occupancy Expense

"Net occupancy expense" is equal to "gross occupancy expense" less rental income. "Gross occupancy expense" includes compensation of bank officers and employees concerned with bank building and related "housekeeping" functions, regardless of whether the bank has a "building department"; supplemental benefits paid or accrued on behalf of such personnel primarily involved with the bank's premises; normal and recurring depreciation charges; ordinary repairs to bank premises and leasehold improvements; and all other current expenses connected with the use of bank premises—heat, electricity, water, janitorial services and supplies, fire insurance, rent paid for premises and parking facilities, interest on mortgages, liens or other encumbrances on bank premises and property, and other tax expenses on bank premises and leasehold improvements. Many banks construct buildings with more space than they currently need. Income derived from rental of this space is offset against the gross occupancy expenses itemized above. Between 1965 and 1977, net occupancy expense declined as a percentage of operating expenses from 5.9 to 3.9 percent.

Furniture and Equipment Expenses

This expense item consists of depreciation; rental costs of office, machines and data processing equipment; ordinary repairs to furniture and office machines, including servicing costs; and taxes on furniture and equipment. Although some students might expect furniture and equipment expenses to be climbing in relative terms because of the increasing use of data processing equipment, such is not the case; between 1965 and 1977, this expense item fell from 3.3 percent to 2.5 percent of operating expense.

Provision for Possible Loan Losses

The "provision for possible loan losses" represents the amount charged against earnings to establish a reserve sufficient to absorb expected loan losses based upon management's knowledge of the loan portfolio as presently constituted. Specifically, in the determination of the adequacy of this reserve, management must continually review problem loans and overall portfolio quality, current and expected economic and financial conditions, loss experience relative to outstanding loans, and examinations by internal and outside auditors and the regulatory authorities. Since 1972, increases in the "provision for possible loan losses" have had a significant impact on income at most banks. As a percentage of operating expenses, this expense item rose from 2.9 percent in 1972 to 6.3 percent in 1975, then declined to 5.2 percent and 4.1 percent in 1976 and 1977, respectively, as economic conditions improved and banks stepped up efforts to control losses.

Other Operating Expenses

"Other operating expenses" contain many costs for items vital to bank operations. Included are fees paid to directors and members of committees for attendance at board or committee meetings; the cost of temporary employees and contracted guards; premiums of fidelity insurance; expenses (except salaries) connected with holdings of real estate other than bank premises; office supplies; the cost of examinations by supervisory authorities; retainer fees; expenses related to the use of automobiles for bank business; losses from counterfeit money, forged checks, net cash shortages, payments of checks over stop payment orders, and similar recurring losses of this type; deposit insurance assessment expenses; advertising costs; and postage. In 1977, "other operating expenses" totaled 12.2 percent for insured banks.

COMPOSITION ANALYSIS OF THE INCOME STATEMENT

Nature and Benefits

In the previous section, we looked at the nature of each item on the income statement. Absolute levels of income and expense items, however, are useful primarily as inputs for making calculations of relative values. Relative values such as those provided through composition analysis provide valuable perspective into a bank's efficiency and profitability.

Composition analysis of the income statement involves calculations of the percentage distribution of operating income and operating expense and a comparison of the distribution with those from previous years and/or with banks of similar asset size or deposit structure. This analytical technique is simple and provides a quick, initial insight into the relative sources of each dollar of operating income and the uses of each dollar of operating expense. Management may use changes in the distribution of income and expenses or deviations from peer group averages as indicators of the need for management action or more detailed analysis with techniques similar to those explained in Chapters 5 and 6. In recent years, the banking regulatory authorities have provided each insured bank with "Comparative Performance Tables," which show the composition of the statement of condition and income statement along with data for similar sized banks.

Table 4-3. Percentage Distribution of Operating Income for Insured Commercial Banks, by Size of Bank, 1977.

Income Item	Total Assets (in Millions)					
	Under 5.0	5.0– 9.9	10.0– 24.9	25.0– 99.9	100.0– 299.9	300 or more
Interest and fees on loans	60.7	63.6	64.7	65.7	64.8	65.4
Interest on balances with banks	1.1	0.6	0.5	0.6	0.7	8.0
Interest on federal funds purchased and security repurchase agreements	4.9	3.9	3.4	2.9	2.7	2.6
Interest on U.S. Treasury securities	14.7	12.5	10.5	9.5	9.5	5.5
Interest on obligations of U.S. agencies and corporations	8.1	7.1	6.0	4.7	4.4	1.5
Interest on obligations of state and political subdivisions	3.5	5.5	7.6	9.0	8.6	4.6
Interest other bonds, notes and debentures	0.7	0.4	0.6	0.7	0.7	1.1
Dividends on stock	0.0	0.1	0.1	0.1	0.1	0.1
Income from direct lease financing	0.0	0.1	0.1	0.2	0.3	1.1
Income from fiduciary activities	0.0	0.2	0.4	0.8	1.9	2.8
Service charges: deposit accounts in domestic offices	2.8	3.1	3.2	3.1	2.6	1.5
Other service charges	2.5	2.3	2.1	1.9	2.3	3.0
Other income	1.1	0.9	0.9	1.0	1.3	2.7
Total operating income	100.0	100.0	100.0	100.0	100.0	100.0

Source: FDIC, unpublished data.

Note: Details may not add to totals due to rounding.

Distribution of Operating Income, by Size of Bank

As might be expected, the distribution of operating income depends upon asset size and deposit structure. Table 4-3 contains the distribution of operating income for banks, by size of bank. As shown in the table, banks with assets above $300 million derive a larger proportion of their income from balances with other banks than do smaller banks, but a smaller proportion from agency, U.S. Treasury, and municipal securities. Loan income and income from fiduciary activities tends to be a higher proportion of operating income.

It is important to understand that deviations of individual bank data from these peer group averages is not necessarily "bad." However, it indicates to analysts and the supervisory authorities that a conscious or unconscious management decision has led to the difference. Management should be able to explain the deviation as it relates to the bank's profitability, liquidity, and capital adequacy goals and to past, present, and expected economic, financial, and competitive trends.

Table 4-4. Percentage Distribution of Operating Expenses for Insured Commercial Banks, by Size of Bank, 1977.

Expense Item	Total Assets (in Millions)					
	Under 5.0	5.0– 9.9	10.0– 24.9	25.0– 99.9	100.0– 299.9	300 or more
Salaries and employee benefits	29.1	25.1	22.8	22.1	22.7	19.8
Interest on CD's over $100,000	2.8	3.4	4.4	6.5	8.6	9.6
Interest on deposits in foreign offices	0.0	0.0	0.0	0.0	0.1	19.8
Interest on other deposits	41.7	45.9	47.4	45.5	40.2	19.1
Expenses for federal funds purchased and securities sold under repurchase agreements	0.4	0.3	0.4	0.8	2.4	8.2
Interest on other borrowed money	0.0	0.1	0.1	0.1	0.2	1.5
Interest on subordinated notes and debentures	0.0	0.1	0.2	0.3	0.6	0.6
Occupancy, furniture, and fixture expenses	6.5	6.4	6.3	6.6	7.3	6.1
Provision for possible loan losses	3.2	3.6	3.5	3.2	3.4	4.6
Other expenses	16.2	15.1	14.9	14.7	14.6	10.8
Total operating expenses	100.0	100.0	100.0	100.0	100.0	100.0

Source: FDIC, unpublished data.

Note: Details may not add to totals due to rounding.

Distribution of Operating Expenses, by Size of Bank

The distribution of operating expenses varies by size of bank much more than does the distribution of operating income. As seen in Table 4-4, interest expense on CD's of $100,000 or more rises directly with asset size, reflecting the dependence of large banks on this interest-sensitive source of funds. Interest on deposits in foreign offices almost is exclusively an expense of banks with assets of $300 million or more. On the other hand, smaller banks have greater expenses for consumer-type savings deposits. Banks in the largest size category also have a much larger "expense for federal funds purchased and securities sold under agreements to repurchase." It also is significant that in 1977, banks with assets above $300 million had the greatest "provision for possible loan losses."

PERCENTAGE INCREASE/DECREASE ANALYSIS OF THE INCOME STATEMENT

Another simple technique of income statement analysis is to calculate the percentage increase or decrease in each income and expense item from the previous year. Analysts sometimes "spread" these percentage changes for five years. The primary benefit from an evaluation of percentage change data is that it suggests areas that need further analysis. For example, interest and fees on loans might increase 15 percent during the year; but was the change due to the increase in the absolute level of loans outstanding, a change in the composition of loans, a change in the level of interest rates and fees charged, or all of the above? Techniques explained in Chapter 6 help to answer such questions.

THREE MEASURES OF BANK INCOME

Table 4-5 contains data on the three primary measures of bank income.

Income before Income Taxes, Security Gains and Losses

"Income before income taxes and security gains and losses" is found by subtracting "operating expenses" from "operating income." Some

Table 4-5. Income, Expenses, and Profits of Insured Commercial Banks, Selected Years, 1960-1977 (Millions of Dollars).

Year	Operating Income	Operating Expenses	Net Operating Income	Net Non-operating Income (+) or Losses (-)[a]	Net Income Before Taxes	Income Taxes[b]	Net Income	Dividends[c]	Net Addition to Capital
1960	10,724	6,933	3,791	-404	3,387	1,384	2,003	832	1,171
1965	16,817	12,486	4,331	-787	3,544	1,029	2,515	1,202	1,313

Year	Operating Income	Operating Expenses	Income Before Income Taxes and Security Gains and Losses	Applicable Income Taxes[d]	Income Before Security Gains and Losses	Net Non-operating Income (+) or Losses (-)[e]	Net Income	Dividends	Net Addition to Capital
1970	34,716	27,589	7,128	2,174	4,954	-117	4,837	2,040	2,797
1973	53,036	44,330	8,707	2,121	6,585	- 6	6,579	2,429	4,150
1974	68,161	58,910	9,251	2,084	7,167	- 76	7,091	2,768	4,323
1975	66,559	57,582	8,977	1,793	7,184	71	7,255	3,032	4,223
1976	80,664	70,750	9,914	2,291	7,623	340	7,843	3,036	4,807
1977	90,069	78,484	11,585	2,829	8,756	142	8,898	3,299	5,599

Source: FDIC, *Annual Reports*; and *Federal Reserve Bulletin*.

Note: Details may not add to totals due to rounding.

[a] Includes net security gains or losses and net recoveries, charge-offs, and transfers to reserves.

[b] Income taxes were $1,864 million in 1970, $1,715 million in 1973, $1,760 million in 1974, $1,727 million in 1975, $2,411 million in 1976 and $2,883 million in 1977.

[c] For 1968 and prior years, "dividends declared on preferred stock" was reported in combination with "interest on capital notes and debentures."

[d] "Applicable income taxes" is an estimate of the tax liabilities that banks would incur if their taxes were based solely on operating income and expenses.

[e] Includes net security gains or losses and net extraordinary charges or credits less minority interest in consolidated subsidiaries.

bankers prefer to call this "net operating income." This measure of income is somewhat similar to "gross profit" for an industrial firm. The concept of the "gross profit margin" will be discussed in Chapter 5.

Income Before Security Gains and Losses and Extraordinary Items

"Income before security gains and losses and extraordinary items" is found by subtracting "applicable income taxes" from the measure of income defined in the paragraph above. "Applicable income taxes" is an estimate of the tax liability that a bank would incur if its taxes were based solely on operating income and expenses; that is, if there were no security gains or losses or extraordinary items. "Applicable income taxes" include federal, state, local, and foreign taxes.

Net Income

"Net income" is found by subtracting "security gains and losses" net of income taxes and "extraordinary items" from "income before security gains and losses and extraordinary items." "Security gains and losses" arise from the sale, exchange, redemption, or retirement of bonds, stocks, and other securities at prices above or below book values. Generally, banks realize security gains during periods of falling interest rates (rising security prices). During the eight year period from 1970 to 1977, banks realized security gains each year except 1970, 1973, and 1974, which were years of tight credit conditions and rising interest rates. Banks are willing to accept these losses because they are fully tax deductible and because of the need to raise funds to meet the legitimate credit demands of valued customers.

Extraordinary items reflect material results of events and transactions, occurring in or related to the current year-to-date, of a character significantly different from the customary activities of the bank. Examples of these gains or losses might include those from (1) the sale of the bank building, (2) gains or losses from a major revaluation of a foreign currency, and (3) significant tax loss carry forwards.

Between 1965 and 1977, operating income for insured banks increased 435.6 percent; however, net income advanced 253.8 percent. The failure of net income to keep pace with operating income is attributed primarily to the increased proportion of time and savings deposits and the rising interest rates on these deposits. A secondary cause of the profits squeeze was the rise since 1973 in the "provision for possible loan losses." Banks were unable to pass along fully increasing expenses in the form of higher interest rates and fees on loans.

5
Traditional Profitability Analysis

In Chapter 1 we examined each of the balance sheet items, and in Chapter 4, we looked at the various income and expense flows. This chapter is the first of two dealing with profitability analysis, which essentially involves relating items on the income statement to those on the statement of condition. "Traditional profitability analysis" refers to the time-honored ways of measuring profitability that bankers have relied upon. In Chapter 6, we shall explore some relatively new techniques to analyze bank profitability.

GROSS PROFIT MARGIN

Industrial firms use the "gross profit margin" as an important measure of profitability. For them, the gross profit margin is equal to sales minus cost of goods sold, divided by sales. This ratio shows what percentage of sales represents profits before making deductions for administrative and other expenses. Viewed over time, the gross profit margin reveals whether or not the firm is maintaining a sufficient mark-up and/or controlling production costs.

In banking, the gross profit margin is found as shown in ratio (1).

$$\text{Gross Profit Margin} = \frac{\text{Operating Income} - \text{Operating Expenses}}{\text{Operating Income}} \quad (1)$$

This ratio provides much the same insights into a bank's operation as it does for an industrial firm. First, the vast majority of operating income is derived primarily from assets such as loans and investments. With respect to loans, banks must price them at a level sufficient to cover expenses and provide for an adequate profit. Of course, loan pricing is conditioned greatly by general monetary and credit conditions, competitive conditions, usury laws, the loan mix, and the ability of lending officers to reflect individual risk levels in interest rates. Yields on investments reflect primarily general monetary and credit conditions, portfolio mix, and the investment officer's ability to make portfolio adjustments in light of expected changes in interest rate levels. Thus, the gross profit margin indicates first the bank's ability to generate income, and second, the bank's ability to control operating expenses. Major operating expenses include interest paid on deposits, personnel costs, and occupancy expenses. Thus, a relative high gross profit margin might reflect managerial ability to keep costs under control.

Table 5-1 contains data on trends in bank gross profit margins, by size of bank. Several conclusions are apparent. Between 1970 and 1977, margins declined sharply in all bank size categories. This trend was caused primarily by (1) a greater proportion of time and savings deposits in the deposit mix; (2) the historically high interest rates on these funds; (3) increases in provision for loan losses; and (4) the

Table 5-1. Gross Profit Margin: Ratio of Income Before Income Taxes and Securities Gains or Losses to Operating Income, for Insured Commercial Banks, by Size of Deposits, 1970–1975, and by Size of Assets, 1976–1977.

Year	Banks with Deposits (Millions of Dollars):					
	Under 5	5–10	10–25	25–100	Over 100	
1970	21.4	21.7	21.2	20.7	20.8	
1971	19.2	19.5	19.0	17.7	17.9	
1972	17.1	18.4	18.5	17.8	17.2	
1973	21.8	21.2	20.4	18.2	15.4	
1974	20.9	20.0	18.9	15.8	n.a.	
1975	14.0	15.3	15.5	13.9	12.1	
Year	Banks with Assets (Millions of Dollars):					
	Under 5	5–9.9	10–24.9	25–99.9	100–299.9	300 or more
1976	12.6	13.5	14.9	14.1	11.7	11.6
1977	13.3	14.3	15.6	15.7	13.6	12.2

Source: FDIC, *Bank Operating Statistics;* and unpublished data.

inability of banks to increase rates on loans commensurate with the increase in costs. It is important to note that margins for banks with deposits or assets above $100 million declined more than those for banks in the $10–25 million and $25–100 million range.

In the current regulatory and competitive environment, it is difficult to envision much improvement in the near future in bank gross profit margins.

NET PROFIT MARGIN

The *net profit margin* for a bank is defined by ratio (2).

$$\text{Net Profit Margin} = \frac{\text{Net Income}}{\text{Operating Income}} \qquad (2)$$

Net income equals "income before income taxes and security gains or losses" less "applicable income taxes" and "security gains or losses." Therefore, a bank's net profit margin depends upon all the factors that influence the gross profit margin plus those that determine "applicable income taxes" and "security gains or losses." "Applicable income taxes" is a function of federal and state corporate income tax rates, the amount of tax exempt interest income, and the investment tax credit. Whether a bank realizes security gains or losses depends largely upon whether interest rates are rising or falling. During years in which rates fall, banks tend to realize security gains. On the other hand, during years in which rates rise, banks usually realize security losses as they sell securities in order to accommodate loan demand.

As seen in Table 5-2, bank net profit margins have fallen for all size categories in the 1970's. Percentage-wise, net profit margins have not declined quite as much as gross profit margins, indicating that the decline in gross profit margins is largely responsible for the decline in net profit margins. Again, net profit margins held up best for banks with deposits or assets between $25 and $100 million. As pointed out earlier, for these sized banks, municipal securities tend to compose a larger percentage of total investments and assets than for smaller banks.

Table 5-2. Net Profit Margin: Ratio of Net Income to Operating Income, for Insured Commercial Banks, by Size of Deposits, 1970-1975, and by Size of Assets, 1976-1977.

Year	Banks with Deposits (Millions of Dollars):					
	Under 5	5-10	10-25	25-100	Over 100	
1970	15.8	15.9	15.4	15.1	14.5	
1971	14.5	15.2	15.2	14.8	14.6	
1972	13.0	14.6	14.9	14.7	13.9	
1973	16.3	16.1	15.6	14.2	12.1	
1974	14.8	14.6	14.2	12.6	n.a.	
1975	10.6	12.2	12.9	12.1	10.5	
Year	Banks with Assets (Millions of Dollars):					
	Under 5	5-9.9	10-24.9	25-99.9	100-299.9	300 or more
1976	10.9	11.7	12.9	12.4	10.7	8.5
1977	11.5	12.3	13.1	13.2	11.8	10.2

Source: FDIC, *Bank Operating Statistics;* and unpublished data.

RETURN ON EQUITY CAPITAL

Return on equity capital is defined by ratio (3).

$$\text{Return on Equity Capital} \ = \ \frac{\text{Net Income}}{\text{Equity Capital}} \qquad (3)$$

For shareholders, this ratio is the most important measure of profitability because it relates net income to the book value of their claims. Equity capital for a bank is the sum of common stock, surplus, and undivided profits. Since net income is a flow over a period (usually a year), it is best to use an average figure for equity capital instead of the year-end total. Many banks with adequate computer capability provide the average daily equity capital total in the annual report. If this is not done, the average of the last and present year-ending amounts for equity capital is satisfactory.

In almost all cases, an increase in return on equity is the result of improved net income. Few banks have reduced equity capital through stock purchases on the open market. A rising return on capital usually is associated with an appreciation in the price of the bank's stock. This improves the prospects of selling additional stock in the market place, and many banks need additional capital to

Table 5-3. Return on Equity: Ratio of Net Income to Equity Capital, for Insured Commercial Banks, by Size of Deposits, 1972-1975, and by Size of Assets, 1976-1977.

	Banks with Deposits (Millions of Dollars):									
Year	Less than 1	1–2	2–5	5–10	10–25	25–50	50–100	100–500	500–1000	1000 or more
1972	6.01	7.37	8.94	10.78	12.15	12.52	12.40	12.29	11.90	11.48
1973	9.09	9.22	11.09	12.55	13.27	13.15	12.53	12.06	12.43	11.98
1974	11.97	10.04	10.30	11.83	12.97	12.27	11.96	11.46	11.65	12.39
1975	2.56	5.23	6.91	9.62	11.58	11.48	11.35	10.53	10.56	12.12

	Banks with Assets (Millions of Dollars):									
Year	Less than 5	5–9.9	10–24.9	25–49.9	50–99.9	100–299.9	300–499.9	500–999.9	1000–4999.9	5000 or more
1976[a]	7.55	9.28	11.41	11.78	11.54	10.63	9.90	10.84	10.26	11.16
1977[a]	6.37	9.09	11.29	12.47	12.21	11.82	11.08	10.42	10.97	10.79

Source: FDIC, *Annual Reports;* and unpublished data.

[a]Ratios based on equity capital reported at end of year.

support growth in assets. Thus, it is easy to see that management and both present and potential shareholders pay very close attention to a bank's return on equity.

Analysis of data in Table 5-3 reveals an interesting pattern of changes in return on equity, by size of bank. In 1972, prior to the severe "money crunch" of 1973-1974, banks in the $25–$100 million deposit range had the highest return on equity. However, in 1973 and 1974, banks with deposits over $1 billion had an increase in return on equity, while banks in the $25–$100 million range suffered declines. An apparent explanation for this divergence is that even with shrinking gross and net profit margins, large banks increased return on equity by expanding assets greatly, financed by the various liability management techniques. As interest rates fell in 1976, the return on equity for banks with assets over $1 billion plummeted, while once again, banks in the $25–$100 million range led all other categories. A sharp rise in the "provision for possible loan losses" and commercial lending rates accounted for part of the decline for banks with assets over $1 billion.

RETURN ON TOTAL ASSETS

There are three profitability ratios for return on total assets.

$$\text{Gross Yield on Total Assets} \ = \ \frac{\text{Operating Income}}{\text{Total Assets}} \quad (4)$$

The ratio of operating income to total assets (4) essentially is an indication of management's ability to generate income. A rising ratio could be the result of a number of factors: more assets employed, earning an explicit income; a portfolio shift to higher yielding assets; an increase in the general level of interest rates; a concerted effort by management to obtain higher yields on loans and other assets; or an increase in fees and income not related to the employment of assets. Thus, a change in the trend in this ratio suggests that the analyst ask a number of questions about management's ability in the area of asset management.

As shown in Table 5-4, from year-to-year, the ratio of operating income to total assets generally does not vary much among size categories. On a year-to-year basis in the 1970's, this ratio moved up

Table 5-4. Gross Yield on Total Assets: Ratio of Operating Income to Total Assets for, Insured Commercial Banks, by Size of Deposits, 1970-1975, and by Size of Assets, 1976-1977.

Year	Banks with Deposits (Millions of Dollars): Under 5	5-10	10-25	25-100	Over 100
1970	6.48	6.42	6.45	6.51	6.51
1971	6.43	6.39	6.40	6.36	6.14
1972	6.27	6.31	6.33	6.32	6.13
1973	6.79	6.77	6.77	6.79	6.87
1974	7.53	7.43	7.37	7.44	n.a.
1975	7.41	7.31	7.26	7.29	7.31

Year	Banks with Assets (Millions of Dollars): Under 5	5-9.9	10-24.9	25-49.9	50-99.9	100-299.9	300-499.9	500-999.9	1000-4999.9	5000 or more
1976[a]	7.18	7.16	7.15	7.17	7.11	7.05	7.06	6.89	6.62	6.61
1977[a]	6.75	7.12	7.21	7.23	7.20	7.09	7.06	6.86	7.21	6.37

Source: FDIC, *Bank Operating Statistics* and *Annual Report,* 1976; and unpublished data.

[a]Ratios are based on assets and liabilities reported at end of year.

sharply between 1972 and 1974, then drifted downward from 1975 through 1977. It is important to know that this ratio has not declined to the pre-1973–1975 level. Essentially, this trend reflects not only the higher general level of interest rate, but also a keener awareness among bankers that yields on assets must be maintained in light of cost pressures from the liability side of the balance sheet and other non-balance sheet expenses.

$$\text{Gross Profit Margin on Total Assets} = \frac{\text{Income Before Taxes and Security Gains and Losses}}{\text{Total Assets}} \quad (5)$$

The ratio of "income before taxes and security gains and losses to total assets" (5) differs from ratio (4) since operating expenses are deducted from operating income in the numerator. Thus, this ratio reflects not only management's ability to generate income, but also its ability to control expenses.

Analysis of Table 5-5 reveals that this ratio in the 1970's has tended to vary directly with the general level of interest rates. It is

Table 5-5. Gross Profit Margin on Total Assets: Ratio of Income Before Taxes and Security Gains or Losses to Total Assets, for Insured Commercial Banks, by Size of Deposits, 1970-1975, and by Size of Assets, 1976-1977.

Year	Banks with Deposits (Millions of Dollars):					
	Under 5	5–10	10–25	25–100	Over 100	
1970	1.41	1.38	1.36	1.34	1.34	
1971	1.22	1.23	1.21	1.12	1.10	
1972	1.09	1.15	1.17	1.12	1.04	
1973	1.45	1.41	1.37	1.23	1.04	
1974	1.53	1.45	1.37	1.16	n.a.	
1975	.99	1.09	1.11	1.00	.87	

Year	Banks with Assets (Millions of Dollars):					
	Under 5	5–9.9	10–24.9	25–99.9	100–299.9	300 or more
1976[a]	.90	.96	1.06	1.04	.83	.79
1977[a]	.79	.90	.96	.99	.86	.73

Source: FDIC, *Bank Operating Statistics* and *Annual Report,* 1976; and unpublished data.

[a]Ratios are based on assets and liabilities reported at end of year.

also important to note that in 1970, there was very little difference in this ratio among size classes; however, over the next six years, these differences widened considerably, with banks in the $10–$100 million range maintaining the highest returns.

$$\text{Net Income on Total Assets} = \frac{\text{Net Income}}{\text{Total Assets}} \quad (6)$$

The ratio of net income to total assets (6) is a good measure of overall profitability and managerial efficiency, although, since the primary financial objective of any firm is to maximize shareholder wealth, the ratio of net income to equity capital would be the superior measure of profitability. The ratio of net income to total assets is determined by the same factors that determine ratio (5) and those factors that determine applicable income taxes, security gains and losses, and extraordinary items. For most banks under $100 million in assets or deposits, the proportion of municipal securities held would be the most important determinant of the relative difference between this ratio and the ratio of income before taxes and security gains and losses to total assets.

Most people unfamiliar with banking tend to overestimate the net return on bank assets by a wide margin. As shown in Table 5-6, the

Table 5-6. Net Income on Total Assets: Ratio of Net Income to Total Assets, for Insured Commercial Banks, by Size of Deposits, 1970-1975, and by Size of Assets, 1976-1977.

Year	Banks with Deposits (Millions of Dollars):				
	Under 5	5–10	10–25	25–100	Over 100
1970	1.04	1.01	.98	.97	.93
1971	.92	.96	.96	.93	.89
1972	.84	.91	.94	.92	.84
1973	1.08	1.07	1.04	.96	.82
1974	1.08	1.06	1.03	.92	n.a.
1975	.75	.87	.92	.87	.75

Year	Banks with Assets (Millions of Dollars):					
	Under 5	5–9.9	10–24.9	25–99.9	100–299.9	300 or more
1976	.84	.93	1.00	.97	.84	.71
1977	.81	.94	1.00	1.01	.88	.74

Source: FDIC, *Bank Operating Statistics;* and unpublished data.

net return on bank assets averaged less than 1 percent in 1977. Banks with over $5 billion in assets averaged only 0.74 percent. Between 1970 and 1977, the net return on assets for banks in the $10–$25 million range was relatively stable, but increased slightly in the tight money years of 1973 and 1974. There was more stability in the net return on assets for banks in the $25–$100 million range.

RETURN ON SPECIFIC ASSETS

Thus far in this chapter, all of the profitability ratios discussed have been aggregate measures and, as such, do not permit an analysis of the influence of the return on specific assets and expenses on specific liabilities. In this section, we shall examine the profitability of three major bank assets: (1) loans, (2) Treasury securities, and (3) municipal securities.

$$\text{Rate of Return on Total Loans} = \frac{\text{Interest and Fees on Loans}}{\text{Total Loans}} \quad (7)$$

Loans are the most important bank earning asset. Therefore, analysis of the ratio of interest and fees earned on loans is a significant measure of management's ability to price its loans and to achieve an optimum loan mix. Improvement in this ratio leads to improvement in every aggregate profitability measure.

As shown in Table 5-7, the return on loans tends to follow the general movement in interest rates. However, in 1976, a year when the prime rate declined, the rate of return on loans increased for all bank size classes. There are at least two possible explanations for this. First, since consumer spending led the economy out of the 1973–1975 recession, the accompanying increase in higher yielding bank installment loans raised overall loan yields, especially for banks under $300 million in assets. The second possibility is that the increase in loan losses and the resulting negative influence on bank earnings underscored the need to reflect the apparent greater risk in loans by increasing loan interest rates and fees. Banks were more reluctant to lend at the prime rate, which is usually given only to business customers of the highest credit quality. In the years ahead, and for the reasons just cited, it seems likely that the rate of return

Table 5-7. Ratio of Return on Loans: Ratio of Interest and Fees on Loans to Total Loans for Insured Commercial Banks, by Size of Deposits, 1970-1975, and by Size of Assets, 1976-1977.

Year	Banks with Deposits (Millions of Dollars): Under 5	5-10	10-25	25-100	Over 100	
1970	7.80	7.82	7.89	7.96	8.12	
1971	7.77	7.76	7.76	7.66	7.45	
1972	7.66	7.66	7.67	7.55	7.29	
1973	8.32	8.29	8.23	8.22	8.36	
1974	9.11	9.01	8.95	9.10	n.a	
1975	8.47	8.58	8.64	8.73	8.72	
Year	Banks with Assets (Millions of Dollars): Under 5	5-9.9	10-24.9	25-99.9	100-299.9	300 or more
1976	8.95	9.05	9.13	9.16	8.98	8.71
1977	9.12	9.25	9.31	9.41	9.22	8.90

Source: FDIC, *Bank Operating Statistics;* and unpublished data.

on loans will not drop in proportion to declines in the prime rate or the general level of interest rates.

$$\text{Rate of Return on Treasury Securities} = \frac{\text{Interest on U.S. Treasury Securities}}{\text{U.S. Treasury Securities}} \quad (8)$$

Treasury securities are held primarily for liquidity purposes; but if market rates are expected to fall and there is the possibility of capital gains, banks will take positions in Treasuries. A bank's yield on Treasuries depends on the general level of interest rates and the maturity distribution of the portfolio. Typically, a portfolio with long-term securities yields more than one with short-term securities. Yields on long-term securities are higher to compensate for their lower liquidity; however, the astute investment manager who is successful in predicting turns in the interest rate cycle may on occasion realize a greater yield on a portfolio that is more heavily weighted with short-term securities.

Table 5-8 shows that the rate of return on Treasuries climbed sharply as the general level of interest rates reached record levels.

Table 5-8. Rate of Return on Treasuries: Interest and Fees on U.S. Treasury Securities to U.S. Treasury Securities at Insured Commercial Banks, by Size of Deposits, 1970-1975, and by Size of Assets, 1976-1977.

Year	Banks with Deposits (Millions of Dollars): Under 5	5–10	10–25	25–100	Over 100	
1970	5.94	5.79	5.69	5.65	5.59	
1971	5.93	5.86	5.84	5.77	5.62	
1972	5.68	5.71	5.70	5.67	5.44	
1973	6.24	6.23	6.18	6.08	5.89	
1974	6.76	6.80	6.71	6.55	n.a.	
1975	6.66	6.63	6.67	6.76	6.64	
Year	Banks with Assets (Millions of Dollars): Under 5	5–9.9	10–24.9	25–99.9	100–299.9	300 or more
1976	7.19	7.19	7.12	7.06	6.84	6.71
1977	6.91	7.00	6.92	6.89	6.76	6.59

Source: FDIC, *Bank Operating Statistics;* and unpublished data.

Yields increased further in 1976 as banks lengthened their portfolio in anticipation of a rally that did not materialize; but this move did increase the current yield on the portfolio. Among bank size classes, there is little difference in yield on Treasuries; however, banks above $100 million tend to realize a slightly lower yield because their holdings generally are short-term.

$$\text{Rate of Return on Municipal Securities} = \frac{\text{Interest on Municipals}}{\text{Municipal Securities}} \quad (9)$$

Essentially, banks hold municipals because they are exempt from federal income tax as well as from state income tax for holders in the state of issue. Banks, by far, hold the largest share of our municipal debt. As with Treasuries, the rate of return on the municipal portfolio depends on the general level of interest rates, the maturity structure, and the investment manager's ability to judge peaks and valleys in the interest rate cycle.

Analysis of data in Table 5-9 reveals that yields have moved up significantly. Data also show that there has been little difference in the return on municipals among bank size classes. However, yields at banks with deposits or assets more than $100 million are slightly lower because these banks tend to prefer shorter-term municipals,

Table 5-9. Rate of Return on Municipals: Interest on Municipals to Municipal Securities at Insured Commercial Banks, by Size of Deposits, 1970-1975, and by Size of Assets, 1976-1977.

Year	Banks with Deposits (Millions of Dollars):				
	Under 5	5-10	10-25	25-100	Over 100
1970	3.62	4.05	4.10	4.20	4.17
1971	3.81	4.16	4.18	4.23	4.12
1972	3.79	4.13	4.20	4.26	4.09
1973	3.50	4.06	4.25	4.42	4.32
1974	3.51	4.20	4.54	4.70	n.a.
1975	3.99	4.58	4.86	4.94	4.90

Year	Banks with Assets (Millions of Dollars):					
	Under 5	5-9.9	10-24.9	25-99.9	100-299.9	300 or more
1976	5.64	5.36	5.17	5.07	4.93	4.95
1977	5.65	5.31	5.16	5.05	4.91	4.86

Source: FDIC, *Bank Operating Statistics;* and unpublished data.

which have a lower return. On the other hand, smaller banks tend to follow a policy of buying municipals in the 10–15 year range and holding them until maturity.

EXPENSE RATIOS

$$\text{Interest Expense Ratio for CD's of \$100,000 or More} = \frac{\text{Interest Paid on CD's of \$100,000 or More}}{\text{CD's of \$100,000 or More}} \quad (10)$$

$$\text{Interest Expense Ratio for Other Domestic Time and Savings Deposits} = \frac{\text{Interest Paid on Other Domestic Time and Savings Deposits}}{\text{Other Time and Savings Deposits}} \quad (11)$$

In the 1970's, the sharp increase in time and savings deposits as a percentage of total deposits, and the rise in the interest rates on these deposits, were the most important reasons for the sharp increase in bank costs. Banks have resorted to high-cost CD's as a way to fund loan demand from valued customers. Banks with pressure on profits typically have an above average ratio of time and savings deposits to total deposits.

Table 5-10. Interest Expense Ratios.

A. Ratio of Interest Paid to Total Time and Savings Deposits, at Insured Commercial Banks, by Size of Deposits, 1970-1975.

Year	Banks with Deposits (Millions of Dollars):				
	Under 5	5-10	10-25	25-100	Over 100
1970	4.41	4.58	4.64	4.77	4.93
1971	4.56	4.70	4.76	4.80	4.77
1972	4.58	4.74	4.76	4.76	4.69
1973	4.77	5.00	5.11	5.28	5.62
1974	5.34	5.61	5.77	6.10	n.a.
1975	5.45	5.63	5.72	5.80	5.88

B. Ratio of Interest Paid to Time Deposits of $100,000 or More, at Insured Commercial Banks, by Size of Assets, 1976-1977.

Year	Banks with Assets (Millions of Dollars):					
	Under 5	5-9.9	10-24.9	25-99.9	100-299.9	300 or more
1976	5.81	6.15	6.46	6.49	6.42	6.28
1977	5.80	5.90	6.01	5.96	5.71	5.49

C. Ratio of Interest Paid to Other Time and Savings Deposits, at Insured Commercial Banks, by Size of Assets, 1976-1977.

Year	Banks with Assets (Millions of Dollars):					
	Under 5	5-9.9	10-24.9	25-99.9	100-299.9	300 or more
1976	5.29	5.38	5.43	5.43	5.27	5.11
1977	5.41	5.44	5.51	5.51	5.41	5.29

Source: FDIC, Bank Operating Statistics; and unpublished data.

Data in Table 5-10 show that rates paid on time and savings deposits advanced sharply in the 1970's, with the largest increase coming in 1974, the peak of the last interest rate cycle. Although a break in the data does not permit a precise comparison, it is obvious that the expense ratio for time and savings deposits retreated very little after this peak. It also is interesting to note that there is little difference in this expense ratio among bank size classes. However, on time deposits of $100,000 or more and for "other time and savings deposits," the interest ratio expense for banks above $300 million in 1976 and 1977 was slightly below that for banks in the $10-$100 million range. The apparent explanation for this is that banks above $300 million generally are the soundest banks and do not have to pay the highest rates for large CD's.

Table 5-11. Ratio of Provision for Loan Losses to Total Loans, at Insured Commercial Banks, by Size of Deposits, 1970-1975, and by Size of Assets, 1976-1977.

Year	Banks with Deposits (Millions of Dollars):					
	Under 5	5-10	10-25	25-100	Over 100	
1970	.28	.27	.26	.22	.21	
1971	.27	.25	.24	.24	.22	
1972	.22	.21	.22	.21	.22	
1973	.20	.21	.22	.23	.22	
1974	.23	.27	.28	.32	n.a.	
1975	.27	.28	.31	.38	.48	

Year	Banks with Assets (Millions of Dollars):					
	Under 5	5-9.9	10-24.9	25-99.9	100-299.9	300 or more
1976	.49	.46	.42	.40	.41	.57
1977	.49	.44	.42	.39	.39	.47

Source: FDIC, *Bank Operating Statistics;* and unpublished data.

$$\text{Provision for Loan Losses Ratio} = \frac{\text{Provision for Loan Losses}}{\text{Total Loans}} \quad (12)$$

Since 1969, the "provision for possible loan losses" has been an operating expense item. From 1970 to 1973, this item averaged less than one-fourth of one percent of total loans (Table 5-11). The 1973–1975 recession and the "shake-out" in the real estate industry were the primary causes of a sharp increase in the provision for loan losses. Although there is a break in the data series, it is clear that banks with deposits or assets above $100 million experienced the greatest loan losses, as measured by the "provision for possible loan losses."

Because of the significant impact that the "provision for loan losses" is having on bank profits, it is important to read the notes and supporting schedules of a bank annual report to determine the type of loans being written off, the trend in losses, and the amount of recoveries. Control of loan losses will be a key to maintaining profitability in the future.

CONCLUDING OBSERVATIONS

In this chapter, we have examined some of the traditional measures of bank profitability. Individual ratios for a bank do not necessarily indicate "good" or "bad" performance. A ratio above or below that for banks of similar size indicates areas of bank policy and performance that should receive further review.

6
Profit Sensitivity Analysis

The primary purpose of this chapter is to explain several more advanced techniques of bank profitability analysis. "Profit sensitivity analysis" refers to the analytical frameworks explained herein, which permit more accurate identification and measurement of the cause and effect factors that influence bank profitability. This chapter applies traditional profit analysis to a hypothetical bank's statement of condition and income statement; explains how to calculate a bank's net interest spread and yield; discusses how to impute changes in interest income and expenses to changes in interest rates and/or levels of earning assets and interest-costing liabilities; examines a model that explains the relationships among the principal determinants of a bank's return on equity capital; traces through this model the effects of various management decisions on a bank's return on equity capital; and explains briefly the impact of these decisions on stock price.

APPLICATION OF TRADITIONAL PROFITABILITY ANALYSIS

Before we proceed to more advanced techniques of bank financial analysis, it would be very helpful for comparative purposes to calculate the traditional profitability measures for a bank. Tables 6-1 and 6-2 contain the statements of condition and income statements, respectively, for Beta National Bank (BNB), a large regional bank. Data for an actual bank were obtained for the years 1976 and

Table 6-1.   Beta National Bank: Statement of Condition, Average Amounts, 1976 and 1977   (Millions of Dollars).

	1977	1976
ASSETS		
Cash and due from banks	722	671
Time deposits in foreign banks	351	250
Money market instruments	20	8
Investment securities		
U.S. Treasury securities	268	245
State and local government securities	259	315
Total investment securities	527	560
Trading account securities	45	40
Federal funds sold and securities purchased under agreements to resell	235	120
Loans and Leases		
Commercial	1,020	951
Consumer	456	362
Mortgage	174	187
Construction	37	40
Foreign	153	137
Other	20	17
Total loans and leases	1,860	1,694
Less allowance for loan and lease losses	18	17
Net loans and leases	1,842	1,677
Premises and equipment	65	66
Other assets	93	82
Total assets	3,900	3,474
LIABILITIES AND SHAREHOLDER'S EQUITY		
Demand deposits	1,330	1,195
Time and savings deposits		
CD's of $100,000 or more	435	495
Domestic time and savings deposits	802	680
Foreign time and savings deposits	496	347
Total time and savings deposits	1,733	1,522
Federal funds purchased and securities sold under agreements to repurchase	498	441
Capital notes	80	83
Other liabilities	73	63
Total liabilities	3,714	3,304
Shareholder's equity	186	170
Total liabilities and shareholder's equity	3,900	3,474

Table 6-2. Beta National Bank: Statement of Income, 1976 and 1977
(Thousands of Dollars).

	1977	1976
Interest and fees on loans and leases		
Commercial	82,772	77,602
Consumer	55,267	44,562
Mortgage	13,137	14,119
Construction	3,075	3,332
Foreign	12,439	11,782
Other	662	867
Total	167,352	152,264
Interest and dividends on investments		
U.S. Treasury securities	18,358	17,273
State and local government securities	24,476	29,988
Total	42,834	47,261
Other interest income		
Time deposits in foreign banks	21,411	15,825
Money market instruments	1,030	556
Trading account securities	3,240	2,988
Total	25,681	19,369
Other income	28,417	26,945
Total operating income	264,284	245,839
Interest expenses		
CD's of $100,000 or more	23,273	27,324
Domestic time and savings deposits	43,308	36,040
Foreign time and savings deposits	30,405	22,277
Total	96,986	85,641
Federal funds purchased and securities sold under agreements to repurchase	27,938	23,130
Less federal funds sold and securities purchased under agreements to resell	12,196	7,012
Net federal funds purchased	15,742	16,118
Capital notes	6,720	6,972
Total interest expenses	119,448	108,371
Allowance for loan and lease losses	9,124	9,587
Other operating expenses	93,095	88,342
Total operating expenses	221,667	206,660
Income before income taxes and security gains and losses	42,617	39,179
Applicable income tax expenses	12,785	11,754
Security gains and losses	103	78
Net income	29,935	27,503

Table 6-3. Beta National Bank: Traditional Profitability Measures, 1976 and 1977 (Thousands of Dollars).

	1977	1976
(1) Gross profit margin		
$= \dfrac{\text{operating income} - \text{operating expense}}{\text{operating income}}$		
1977 = (264,284 – 221,667)/ 264,284	16.13%	
1976 = (245,839 – 206,660)/ 245,839		15.94%
(2) Net profit margin		
= net income/operating income		
1977 = 29,935/264,284	11.33%	
1976 = 27,503/245,839		11.19%
(3) Return on equity capital		
= net income/equity capital		
1977 = 29,935/186,000	16.09%	
1976 = 27,503/170,000		16.18%
(4) Gross yield on total assets		
= operating income/total assets		
1977 = 264,284/3,900,000	6.78%	
1976 = 245,839/3,474,000		7.08%
(5) Gross profit margin on total assets		
$= \dfrac{\text{income before tax and security gains or losses}}{\text{total assets}}$		
1977 = 42,617/3,900,000	1.09%	
1976 = 39,179/3,474,000		1.13%
(6) Net income on total assets		
= net income/total assets		
1977 = 29,935/3,900,000	0.77%	
1976 = 27,503/3,474,000		0.79%
(7) Rate of return on loans		
$= \dfrac{\text{interest and fees on loans}}{\text{total loans}}$		
1977 = 167,352/1,860,000	9.00%	
1976 = 152,264/1,694,000		8.99%
(8) Rate of return on Treasury securities		
= interest earned on Treasury securities/Treasury securities		
1977 = 18,358/268,000	6.85%	
1976 = 17,273/245,000		7.05%

Table 6-3. Beta National Bank: Traditional Profitability Measures, 1976 and 1977 (Thousands of Dollars). Continued

	1977	1976
(9) Rate of return on municipal securities = tax adjusted interest on municipal securities/municipal securities		
1977 = 24,476/259,000	9.45%	
1976 = 29,988/315,000		9.52%
(10) Interest expense ratio for CD's of $100,000 or more = interest paid on CD's/CD's of $100,000 or more		
1977 = 23,273/435,000	5.35%	
1976 = 27,324/495,000		5.52%
(11) Interest expense ratio for other domestic time and savings deposits = interest on other domestic time and savings deposits/domestic time and savings deposits		
1977 = 43,308/802,000	5.40%	
1976 = 36,040/680,000		5.30%
(12) Provision for loan losses ratio = provision for loan losses/total loans		
1977 = 9,124/1,860,000	0.49%	
1976 = 9,587/1,694,000		0.57%

Source: Tables 6-1 and 6-2.

1977, then altered in a number of ways to disguise the bank's identity. However, most of the fundamental changes in the statements of condition and income statements were retained to show how the bank's statements and profitability changed in response to management's decisions and economic, financial, and competitive influences.

Table 6-3 contains a summary of the profitability measures for BNB and shows how to calculate these ratios using data in Tables 6-1 and 6-2. As seen in Table 6-3, total operating income increased from $245,839,000 in 1976 to $264,284,000 in 1977, and both gross and net profit margins rose in 1977. However, between 1976 and 1977, the bank's gross yield on total assets declined from 7.08 to 6.78 percent; the gross profit margin on total assets fell from 1.13 to 1.09 percent; and the return on equity capital declined from

16.18 to 16.09 percent. How can a bank increase its operating income and its efficiency in producing profits from that income stream, yet decrease the gross profit margin on assets and (more importantly) the bank's return on equity capital? The return on loans was virtually unchanged, while the rate of return on municipals and U.S. Treasury securities fell. At first glance, the change in the rate of return and the proportion of assets in these two investments do not seem large enough to account for the decline in profit on total assets. Moreover, the provision for loan losses declined in 1977. Another question is: Did changes in the sources of funds to finance growth in bank assets from $3,474,000,000 in 1976 to $3,900,000,000 in 1977 adversely affect profitability? Traditional measures of profitability indicate only that changes have occurred, but other analytical techniques are needed to determine causal relationships.

SPREAD ANALYSIS

The first of the more advanced bank financial analysis techniques that we will examine is *spread analysis*. Essentially, this method measures and examines the causes of changes in the difference between gross interest and fees received on earning assets and the gross interest paid on interest-costing liabilities. This difference in dollars is called the *net interest spread* and, in percentage terms, the *net interest yield*. Non-financial businesses have used spread and margin concepts for centuries. When a merchant purchases goods, he adds to the cost of goods an amount to cover expenses and to earn a reasonable profit, and the difference between the cost of goods and the selling price is called a "spread" or "margin." Banks act in a similar manner, but they deal in dollars and not goods. Banks acquire funds principally by issuing claims on themselves, such as CD's, time and savings deposits, and federal funds purchased; in return, they promise to pay interest. Banks acquire assets, such as loans and investments, for which they receive interest and fees. The difference between what the banks pay for funds and what they get for funds is a "spread." How is this spread calculated?

Data in BNB's statement of condition and income statement have been rearranged in Table 6-4. The first step in spread analysis is to

Table 6-4. Beta National Bank: Average Balance Sheet Level, Statement of Income, and Yields and Rates on a Fully Taxable Equivalent Basis, 1976 and 1977 (Balance Sheet—Millions of Dollars; Income and Expense—Thousands of Dollars.)

	1977			1976		
	Average Balance Sheet Level	Income or Expense	Yield/Rate	Average Balance Sheet Level	Income or Expense	Yield/Rate
Earning assets:						
Time deposits in foreign banks	351	21,411	6.10%	250	15,825	6.33%
Money market instruments	20	1,030	5.15	8	556	6.95
Investment securities						
U.S. Treasury securities	268	18,358	6.85	245	17,273	7.05
State and local government debt	259	24,476	9.45	315	29,988	9.52
Total investment securities	527	42,834	8.13	560	47,261	8.44
Trading account securities	45	3,240	7.20	40	2,988	7.47
Loans and leases						
Commercial	1,020	82,772	8.11	951	77,602	8.16
Consumer	456	55,267	12.12	362	44,562	12.31
Mortgage	174	13,137	7.55	187	14,119	7.55
Construction	37	3,075	8.31	40	3,332	8.33
Foreign	153	12,439	8.13	137	11,782	8.60
Other	20	662	3.31	17	867	5.10
Total loans and leases	1,860	167,352	9.00	1,694	152,264	8.99
Total earning assets	2,803	235,867	8.41	2,552	218,894	8.58
Remaining assets:						
Cash and due from banks	722			671		
Federal funds sold and securities purchased under agreements to resell	235			120		
Premises and equipment	65			66		

Table 6-4. Beta National Bank: Average Balance Sheet Level, Statement of Income, and Yields and Rates on a Fully Taxable Equivalent Basis, 1976 and 1977 (Balance Sheet—Millions of Dollars; Income and Expense—Thousands of Dollars). Continued

	1977			1976		
	Average Balance Sheet Level	Income or Expense	Yield/Rate	Average Balance Sheet Level	Income or Expense	Yield/Rate
Other assets	93			82		
Allowance for loan losses	-18			-17		
Other operating income		28,417			26,945	
Total assets	3,900			3,474		
Total operating income		264,284			245,839	
Liabilities and equity:						
Interest costing liabilities and time and savings deposits						
CD's of $100,000 or more	435	23,273	5.35	495	27,324	5.52
Domestic time and savings	802	43,308	5.40	680	36,040	5.30
Foreign time and savings	496	30,405	6.13	347	22,277	6.42
Total time and savings	1,733	96,986	5.60	1,522	85,641	5.63
Capital notes	80	6,720	8.40	83	6,972	8.40
Federal funds purchased	498	27,938	5.61	441	23,130	5.24
Less federal funds sold	235	12,196	5.19	120	7,012	5.84
Net federal funds	263	15,742	5.99	321	16,118	5.02
Total interest costing liabilities	2,076	119,448	5.75	1,926	108,731	5.65
Net interest income/spread		116,419	2.66		110,163	2.93
Demand deposits	1,330			1,195		
Other liabilities	73			63		
Adjustment for federal funds sold	235			120		
Total liabilities	3,714			3,304		

Table 6-4. Beta National Bank: Average Balance Sheet Level, Statement of Income, and Yields and Rates on a Fully Taxable Equivalent Basis, 1976 and 1977 (Balance Sheet—Millions of Dollars; Income and Expense—Thousands of Dollars). Continued

	1977			1976	
	Average Balance Sheet Level	Income or Expense	Yield/Rate	Average Balance Sheet Level	Income or Expense	Yield/Rate
Stockholder's equity	186			170		
Total liabilities and equity	3,900			3,474		
Other operating expenses		93,095			88,342	
Allowances for loan losses		9,124			9,587	
Total operating expenses		221,667			206,660	
Net operating income		42,617			39,179	
Applicable income tax expenses		12,785			11,754	
Securities gains		103			78	
Net income		29,935			27,503	

identify earning assets; that is, those that yield an explicit income stream. These are grouped in the top section of Table 6-4. Second, from the income statement, identify the income realized from each earning asset. Finally, express this annual income as a percentage of the average earning asset. For example, in 1977, the yield on time deposits in foreign banks was 6.10 percent ($21,411,000/$351,000,000). In all, BNB had earning assets of $2,803,000,000, which yielded total income of $235,867,000 for a gross yield of 8.41 percent.

Turning to the cost of funds side, each interest-costing liability is identified, and the annual outlay is matched with it. Dividing this outlay by the average balance sheet amount gives the cost in percentage terms. For example, in 1977, BNB had $435,000,000 in CD's of $100,000 or more. The annual interest cost on these funds was $23,273,000 for an average cost of 5.35 percent. (It should be noted that BNB was a net purchaser of federal funds, so federal funds sold was netted against federal funds purchased.) In all, BNB had $2,076,000,000 in interest-costing liabilities with an explicit interest cost of $119,448,000 or 5.75 percent.

The net yield, or difference between the rate earned on income producing assets and the rate cost of interest-costing liabilities was 8.41 percent minus 5.75 percent or 2.66 percent. This is in comparison with a spread of 3.03 percent in 1976, indicating that market forces on interest rates, both earned and received, reduced bank profitability. Although the yield on assets moved closer to the cost of funding these assets, the dollar spread increased from $110,163,000 in 1976 to $116,419,000 in 1977. Thus, it appears that BNB's management responded to the profit squeezing forces of a decline in asset yields and an increase in liability interest costs by increasing the dollar amount of the spread. How was this accomplished?

RATE/LEVEL ANALYSIS

Data in   Table 6-4 is rearranged in Table 6-5 to show both the absolute and percentage changes in each type of income and expense flow beside each earning asset and interest-costing liability, respectively. For example, the change in income on time deposits was $5,586,000 ($21,411,000 minus $15,825,000), and the percentage

Table 6-5. Beta National Bank: Change in Income and Expense and Change in Balance Sheet Levels, 1976-1977 (Income and Expense—Thousands of Dollars; Balance Sheet—Millions of Dollars).

	Changes in Income Statements		Changes in Balance Sheet Levels		
	Amount	Percent	Sources of Funds	Uses of Funds	Percent
Earning assets:					
Time deposits in foreign banks	5,586	35%		101	40%
Money market instruments	474	85		12	150
Investment securities					
U.S. Treasury securities	1,085	6		23	9
State and local government securities	-5,512	-18	56		-18
Total investment securities	-4,427	- 9	33		- 6
Trading account securities	252	8		5	12
Loans and leases					
Commercial	5,170	7		69	7
Consumer	10,705	24		94	26
Mortgage	-982	7	13		- 7
Construction	-257	- 8	3		- 8
Foreign	657	6		16	12
Other	-205	-24		3	18
Total loans and leases	15,088	10		166	10
Total earning assets	16,973	8		251	9
Remaining assets:					
Cash and due from banks				51	8
Allowance for loan losses			1		- 6
Premises and equipment			1		2
Other assets				11	13
Other operating income	1,472	5			
Total assets				426	12
Total operating income	18,445	8			
Liabilities and equity:					
Interest costing liabilities and time and savings deposits					
C.D.'s of $100,000 or more	-4,051	-15		60	- 12
Domestic time and savings	7,268	20	122		18
Foreign time and savings	8,128	36	149		43
Total time and savings	11,345	13	211		14
Capital notes	-252	- 4		3	- 4
Federal funds purchased	4,808	21	57		13
Less federal funds sold	5,184	74		115	96
Net Federal funds purchased	-376	- 2		58	- 18
Total interest costing liabilities	10,717	10	150		8

Table 6-5. Beta National Bank: Change in Income and Expense and Change in Balance Sheet Levels, 1976–1977 (Income and Expense—Thousands of Dollars; Balance Sheet—Millions of Dollars). Continued

| | Changes in Income Statements | | Changes in Balance Sheet Levels | | |
	Amount	Percent	Sources of Funds	Uses of Funds	Percent
Demand deposits			135		11
Other liabilities			10		16
Total liabilities			410		12
Stockholder's equity			16		9
Total liabilities and equity			426		12
Other operating expense	4,753	5			
Allowances for loan losses	–463	–5			
Total operating expense	15,007	7			
Net operating income	3,438	9			
Income tax	1,031	8			
Securities gains	25	32			
Net income	2,432	9			
Total sources and uses			563	563	

change was 35 percent ($5,586,000/$15,825,000). This increase was caused, in part, by an increase in the amount invested of $101,000,000 ($351,000,000 minus $250,000,000), which works out to a 40 percent ($101,000,000/$250,000,000) increase in the level or amount invested. The $101,000,000 increase in level is in Table 6-5 as a "use" of funds; that is, as a net investment in that account during the year.[1] On the other hand, investment in state and local government securities decreased by $5,512,000. The decrease in the gross yield on this asset category from 9.52 to 9.45 percent was partially responsible for the decrease in income. However, most of the decrease in dollar income on municipals must be imputed to the $56,000,000 net reduction in investment in these securities. This decrease is recorded as a "source" of funds: i.e., this disinvestment provided funds for other assets or a reduction in liabilities.

To illustrate a change on the cost side, the interest cost on domestic time and savings deposits increased $7,268,000. This change was

[1] Uses of funds are to increase assets or to decrease liabilities; sources of funds result from increases in liabilities or decreases in assets.

partly due to the $122,000,000 increase in these deposits—a source of funds, and partly due to a rise in the interest rate cost from 5.30 to 5.40 percent.

Changes in the sources and uses of funds in 1977 totaled $563,000,000. Sources of funds came primarily from an increase in demand deposits, domestic and foreign time and savings deposits, and the reduction in municipals. Principal uses of the $563,000,000 were to increase time deposits in foreign banks, to increase commercial and consumer loans, and to sell federal funds.

At this point, it should be clear that changes in interest rates and in levels of the accounts influenced the profitability of the bank. The effects of the rate and level on the dollar amount of income and expense can be separated. The dollar return on an asset for a year can be expressed as its yield times the amount invested, and can be depicted as the area of a rectangle with height representing yield and length representing the amount invested. As shown in Part A of Figure 6-1, in Year 1, $1,000 is invested at 8 percent. Interest earnings of $80 are shown in the area of the rectangle. Part B, shows that in Year 2, the interest rate increases to 10 percent, with interest earnings rising to $100. The $20 additional interest is due entirely to the change in yield, and can be determined as the difference in the yield times the amount invested, or $(R2 - R1)(L1) = (.1 - .08)(1,000) = \$20$.

During the year, if there had also been an increase of $250 invested, the interest on the investment would have been $(R2)(L2) = (.10)(1,250) = \$125$; an increase of $45 in interest over that of Year 1. What amount was due to a rise in yield, and what portion of the $45 was due to an increase in the amount invested? The increase in interest due to the increase in yield is $(R2 - R1)(L1)$ or $20. The increase in interest due to the increase in the amount invested is shown in Part C to be $(R2)(L2 - L1) = (.10)(1,250 - 1,000) = \$25$. The results are summarized below.

Change due to yield change	$20 = (R2 - R1)(L1)$
Change due to asset change	$\underline{\$25} = (R2)(L2 - L1)$
Total change	$45

The change in interest from 1976 to 1977 divided between the yield and asset level causes is shown in Table 6-6. The yield on assets

A. Beginning period, Year 1.

Rate

$R_1 = 8\%$

Total
interest = $80

Level $1,000
               L_1

B. Increase in yield in Year 2.

Rate

$R_2 = 10\%$ Added
                interest = $20
$R_1 = 8\%$

Total
interest = $100

Level $1,000
               L_1

C. Increase in yield and level in Year 2.

Rate

$R_2 = 10\%$ Added
                interest = $20
$R_1 = 8\%$

Total   Added
interest = $125   interest =
                             $25

Level $1,000 $1,250
               L_1 L_2

Figure 6-1. Rate/Level Analysis.

Table 6-6. Beta National Bank: Allocation of Income and Expenses to Changes in Balance Sheet Levels and Yield/Rates, 1976-1977. (Thousands of Dollars).

	Increase (Decrease) in Income and Expenses Due to Change in:		
	Average Level $	Yield/Rate $	Total $
Operating income from earning assets:			
Time deposits in foreign banks	6,161	-575	5,586
Money market instruments	618	-144	474
Investment securities			
U.S. Treasury securities	1,575	-490	1,085
State and local government securities	-5,292	-220	-5,512
Trading account securities	360	-108	252
Loans and leases			
Commercial	5,646	-476	5,170
Consumer	11,393	-688	10,705
Mortgage	-982	-0-	-982
Construction	-249	-8	-257
Foreign	1,300	-643	657
Other	99	-304	-205
Total	20,629	-3,656	16,973
Interest expense on interest costing liabilities:			
Time and savings deposits			
CD's of $100,000 or more	-3,210	-841	-4,051
Domestic time and savings	6,588	680	7,268
Foreign time and savings	9,134	-1,006	8,128
Capital notes	-252	-0-	-252
Federal funds purchased	3,198	1,610	4,808
Less federal funds sold	-5,968	-784	-5,184
Total	9,490	1,227	10,717
Change in net interest income	11,139	-4,883	6,256

and interest cost of liabilities is being examined, so only earning assets and interest costing liabilities are presented.

Returning to the BNB example, the revenue from earning assets increased $16,973,000 in 1977 over 1976. The yield on each separate type of asset either was the same or lower in 1977. The impact of the overall lower yields was to lower the interest earned by $3,656,000. But the total level of earning assets increased by $251,000,000, which, by itself, raised interest earned by $20,629,000. The net effect of the increase in earning assets and the decrease in yields was to raise the interest earned on earning assets by $16,973,000 to $235,867,000. Totals are found by adding the amounts in each asset account.

Because of the importance of loans in the total earnings picture, it would be useful to examine the impact of a change in portfolio composition. The category "loans and leases" had an increase in interest earned in 1977 due to a rise in yields, yet the yield of each component was the same or lower, since during this period, funds were shifted from lower yielding uses (e.g., mortgage loans) into higher yielding loans (e.g., consumer loans). Although the yield on consumer loans fell from 12.31 to 12.12 percent, the yield on total loans and leases rose because funds that were yielding 7.55 percent were shifted to assets earning 12.12 percent. In sum, interest income increased $16,973,000, the net result of a $20,629,000 increase due to a rise in the level of earning assets and a $3,656,000 decrease because of a decline in interest rates. On the cost side, an increase in the level of liabilities added $9,490,000 to costs, while an increase in interest rates added $1,227,000 to costs. The bottom line reflects the net result of all of these forces—a $6,256,000 increase in net interest income. In spite of this increase, total assets increased more percentage-wise, thus causing a decline in net income on assets.

For management and outsiders, rate/level analysis is an invaluable tool of bank financial analysis. With this technique, bankers can evaluate past and future policy decisions in both asset and liability management, and outsiders such as investors and banking regulatory authorities can evaluate managerial ability in light of economic, financial, and competitive conditions.

A MODEL TO EXPLAIN RETURN ON EQUITY CAPITAL

The gross profit margin on assets for BNB was 1.09 percent in 1977, and the return on equity capital was 16.09 percent. How can assets earning 1.09 percent before income tax provide shareholders with an after tax rate of return on equity capital of 16.09 percent?

The return on equity capital is defined in Chapter 5 as a net income divided by equity capital, or $29,935,000/$186,000,000 = 16.09 percent. The purpose of this section is to bring together all the

Figure 6-2. Factors Influencing the Return on Equity Capital.

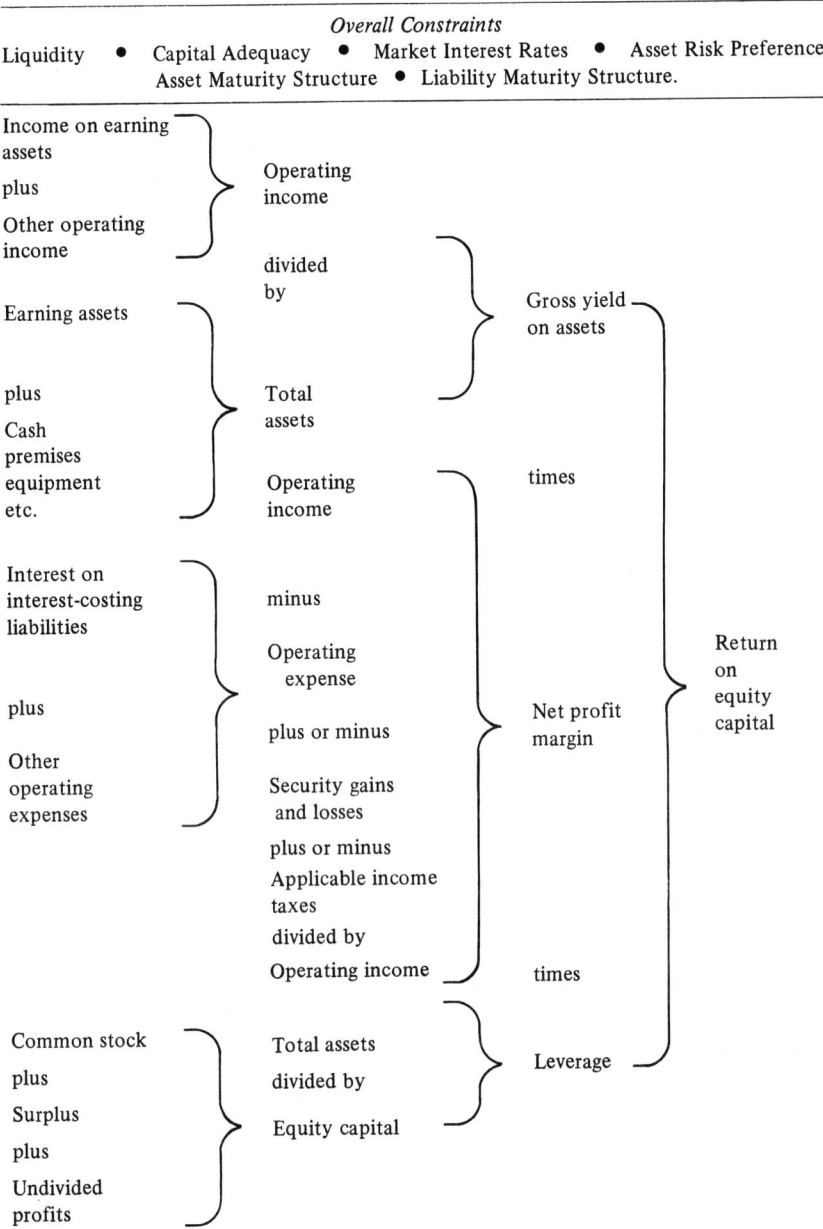

Overall Constraints

Liquidity   •   Capital Adequacy   •   Market Interest Rates   •   Asset Risk Preferences
Asset Maturity Structure • Liability Maturity Structure.

Income on earning
assets

plus

Other operating
income

Operating
income

divided
by

Earning assets

plus

Cash
premises
equipment
etc.

Total
assets

Operating
income

Gross yield
on assets

times

Interest on
interest-costing
liabilities

minus

Operating
expense

plus

Other
operating
expenses

plus or minus

Security gains
and losses

plus or minus
Applicable income
taxes

divided by

Operating income

Net profit
margin

times

Return
on
equity
capital

Common stock

plus

Surplus

plus

Undivided
profits

Total assets

divided by

Equity capital

Leverage

major factors influencing return on equity capital into one explanatory framework.

The return on equity capital can be viewed as the product of three measures: the *gross yield on assets* times the *net profit margin* times *leverage*. Although these variables are interrelated, the gross yield on assets, measured by operating income divided by total assets, is more closely identified with the revenue producing ability of the bank. This measure, which is similar to the "turnover of total assets" (sales/total assets) used in the analysis of non-financial firms, tends to increase as market interest rates on earning assets rise and as service charges and other fee income increases. The net profit margin is equal to operating income less operating expenses, less applicable income taxes, plus or minus security gains and losses, all divided by operating income. This measure rises with management's ability to acquire and utilize funds and operate the bank efficiently. The third measure, leverage, is defined as total assets divided by equity capital. The return on equity capital usually increases if more assets are financed profitably with non-shareholder funds, but risk to the stockholder also rises. These three measures, along with their basic determinants, are illustrated in Figure 6-2.

The gross yield on assets, net profit margin, leverage, and return on equity capital for BNB in 1976 and 1977 are calculated and shown in Figure 6-3. This method of analysis proves the rate of return of equity capital of 16.09 percent shown earlier and adds an element of its own, the effect of the increase in leverage in 1977. Total assets increased 12 percent and equity capital increased 9 percent, making the measurement of leverage rise from 20.44 to 20.97. The gross yield in 1977 combined with the net profit margin in 1977 and the leverage factor of 1976 produced a rate of return on equity capital of 15.69 percent. The increase in leverage and the additional risk exposure of lower capital adequacy reduced the impact of the lower earnings on assets and spreads.

Impact of Changes in Market Rates of Return on Equity Capital

How sensitive is the rate of return on equity capital to changes in market rates of interest? The analysis presented here is not sufficiently

	1977	1976
Gross yield on assets (Operating Income/Total Assets)	.0678	.0708
times		
Net profit margin (Net income/Operating income)	.1133	.1119
times		
Leverage (Total assets/Equity capital)	20.97	20.44
equals		
Return on equity capital	.1609	.1618
	or	or
	16.09 %	16.18 %

Note: Details do not multiply to total due to rounding.

Figure 6-3. Beta National Bank: Components of Return on Equity Capital.

elborate to fully answer this question, but a satisfactory start may be made. The method presented in Figure 6-3 indicates that if the gross yield were to rise 10 percent, then the return on equity capital would rise 10 percent (if there were no changes in the net profit margin or in leverage). The model does not attempt to determine how much the gross yield would rise if market rates were to rise 10 percent. The degree of interest rate sensitivity of the assets (and of the liabilities) would have to be known to answer that question precisely. The degree of sensitivity would depend primarily upon the extent to which loan rates were tied to market rates, the maturity of investments, the amount of turnover in the portfolio, and other yield and interest cost factors.

Impact of Changes in risk. The impact of risk on return on equity capital occurs in many places in Figure 6-2. The impact of adding risk by increasing leverage already has been noted. The gross income on assets times the net profit margin equals the net income on assets. Shifting funds from lower risk and lower yielding assets to higher risk assets with higher promised yields will tend to raise the yield on assets. The rate of return on equity capital would tend to rise if the net profit margin remains the same. However, that margin may rise if the higher risk assets require an increase in operating expenses.

Impact of Changes in Liquidity. Changes in liquidity may be made by increasing the portion of the portfolio invested in low yielding, but relatively riskless, securities, thus increasing the portion of cash assets to total assets. This decrease in earning assets relative to total assets also would tend to reduce the gross yield on assets and, therefore, the return on equity capital.

Impact of Changes in Capital. Changes in equity capital have been considered above under the change in risk heading. Changes in debt capital may have an impact on return on equity capital by increasing capital adequacy which increases the ability to have a less liquid asset mix and to invest in securities that have higher risk and higher yields. As a relatively rate insensitive method of raising funds, future earnings will be higher if capital is increased now and market rates rise in the future.

Summary of Changes. The expected effects of a list of changes is shown in Figure 6-4. Not all the results are certain, as some of the changes may have multiple effects. A "+" is used to indicate that the profit measure probably would rise, a "−" indicates a fall, a "0" indicates no change, and a "+/−" indicates possible conflicting effects.

IMPACT OF ASSET/LIABILITY MANAGEMENT DECISIONS ON STOCK PRICE

In situations when it is possible for management to take actions that would raise the anticipated future stream of earnings for common shareholders without causing an increase in risk, or when earnings would be the same with less risk, or when earnings would be available sooner, it is obvious that shareholder wealth would increase. It is in situations when a decision may raise earnings and risk, or may reduce current earnings while promising more in the future, or may lower earnings and lower risk, that troubles arise. Clearly, it is not in the best interest of shareholders to follow policies that attempt to

CHANGE	EFFECT				
	Gross Yield on Assets	Net Profit Margin on Assets	Leverage	Return on Equity Capital	Risk
(1) An increase in market yields on assets.	+	+	0	+	0
(2) An increase in interest cost on interest costing liabilities.	0	–	0	–	0
(3) A decrease in liquidity caused by: (a) substitution of earning assets for cash assets; or	+	+	0	+	+
(b) investing in higher yielding assets carrying more risk.	+	+/–	0	+/–	+
(4) Increasing leverage (% Δ in assets > % Δ in share-holder's equity).	0	0	+	+	+

Figure 6-4. Summary of Cause and Effect Relationship in the Bank Return on Equity Model.

maximize earnings without regard to the risk of greater leverage or the risk of lower liquidity. Also, if current market rates are lower on short term funds than on longer term funds, the decision to raise short term funds may increase earnings now at the expense of earnings in the future. In the future, liquidity needs may have to be financed at extremely high short term rates. This point is that the analysis of changes over time should consider not just the rate of return on equity capital, but the impact of the risk on the market's perception of what the bank's shares are worth in light of the greater risk.

7
Early Warning Signals of Changes in Bank Financial Conditions

INFLUENCE OF RECENT BANK FAILURES

The failure of the U.S. National Bank of San Diego on October 18, 1973 and Franklin National Bank of New York on October 8, 1974 shocked the banking and financial community as no other events have since the Great Depression. Prior to these failures, bankers, bank regulatory authorities, and informed people in the business community generally believed that, in a world of FDIC insurance and an enlightened Federal Reserve, "only small unit banks in rural communities could fail." However, the collapse of U.S. National and Franklin National shattered this belief; people began to say "if these banks can fail, any bank can fail." The term "problem bank" became common in the financial press, and rumors flew left and right that this or that money market or regional bank was on the "problem list."[1]

This realization that banks can fail provoked the obvious question: How can a bank in deteriorating financial condition be spotted? Holders of bank stocks, corporate cash managers with uninsured

---

[1] A *problem bank* is "one that has violated a banking law or regulation or engaged in an unsafe and unsound banking practice to an extent that the present or future solvency of the bank is in question." Joseph F. Sinkey, Jr. and David A. Walker, "Problem Banks: Identification and Characteristics," Bank Administration Institute, *Journal of Bank Research*, Winter 1975, p. 209.

deposits, bankers, and bank regulatory authorities were most inter-
rested in the answer to this question.   Financial economists with
the bank regulatory authorities and academic economists launched
extensive studies into the characteristics of problem banks and possible
early warning signals to detect banks that are deteriorating.   The
bank regulatory authorities particularly wanted to develop early
warning signals, since, if deterioration was detected, supervision and
examination could be increased and perhaps failures could be pre-
vented.   Early warning signals could improve efficiency in bank
examination because additional efforts could be directed toward the
"vulnerable" banks and less toward the "resistant" banks.   Elaborate
statistical functions have been developed toward this end.   However,
these models are not readily accessible to those in the private sector.
The purpose of this chapter is to identify those early signals that
financial economists have determined tend to be related to deteriorating financial conditions.   Most of these signals have been discussed
in previous chapters; however, since spotting a deteriorating bank is
an important objective of bank financial analysis, it would be useful
to highlight and discuss these early warning signals.

CHARACTERISTICS OF PROBLEM BANKS

In 1975, Joseph F. Sinkey, Jr. and David A. Walker, financial economists with the FDIC, published one of the first in-depth studies
on problem banks.[2]   Taking the January 1973 "problem list" of 210
banks, in terms of characteristics, they found that 198 had deposits
of less than $50 million, and only 12 had deposits above this mark.
In terms of structure, 162 were unit banks; none had more than 5
branches.   With respect to specific problems at the 210 banks, 206
banks had "poor asset condition due to present and/or prior management," and 69 banks had "prior and/or present self-serving management."[3]   Other problems, such as defalcation and/or irregularities,
bad economy, out-of-area loans, and "other" reasons were cited only
43 times.   Given the preponderance of problems that were imputed
to management weaknesses, the economists then proceded to design

[2]Sinkey and Walker, *op. cit.*

[3]*Ibid.*, p. 210. Many banks on the list had multiple problems.

Table 7-1. Financial Ratios Indicating Differences Between Problem and Non-problem Banks.

1. *Capital Adequacy*
   (a) Capital/Total Assets
   (b) Capital/Risk Assets
   (c) Excess Capital Funds/Risk Assets
   (d) Loans/Capital

2. *Liquidity*
   (a) U.S. Treasury Securities/Assets

3. *Loan Characteristics*
   (a) Loans/Total Assets
   (b) Commercial and Industrial Loans/Loans
   (c) Interest and Fees on Loans/Operating Income

4. *Efficiency*
   (a) Operating Expense/Operating Income

5. *Rates of Return*
   (a) Net Income/Total Assets
   (b) Net Income/Capital

Source: Joseph F. Sinkey, Jr. and David A. Walker, "Problem Banks: Identification and Characteristics," Bank Administration Institute, *Journal of Bank Research,* Winter 1975, pp. 214 and 216.

Note: Capital = total capital accounts. Risk assets = total assets – cash – U.S. Treasury securities. Excess capital funds = total capital accounts – preferred and common stock (par value). Loans = total loans and discounts. Reserves = total reserves for bad debt losses and loans.

a research project that would indirectly measure the impact of managerial decisions.

Briefly summarizing the study, each of the 62 problem banks that were added to the problem list in 1972 were matched with a non-problem bank of similar size and structure. A detailed analysis of the operating and financial characteristics of the problem and non-problem banks for 1969,1970, and 1971 was made to determine significant statistical differences between the two groups. A summary of the significant ratios for 1971 is shown in Table 7-1. As seen in the table, the ratios are grouped under five classifications: (1) capital adequacy, (2) liquidity, (3) loan characteristics, (4) efficiency, and (5) rates of return.

Capital Adequacy

First, under capital adequacy, problem banks had *lower* average ratios of capital to total assets and capital to risk assets. Another measure of capital adequacy was the ratio of excess capital to risk assets, where excess capital is defined as total capital accounts, minus the par value of preferred and common stocks. This ratio was significantly lower for problem banks in 1971 (but, interestingly, was not significant for balance sheet data analyzed for these banks for the years 1969 and 1970). Finally, the ratio of loans to capital plus reserves was significantly higher for problem banks and also was adjudged to be perhaps the most important capital ratio to indicate deterioration in financial condition.

Liquidity

A priori, one would expect problem banks to have liquidity pressures. Of all the liquidity ratios tested, only in the ratio of U.S. Treasury securities to total assets was there a significant difference between the two groups of banks. Between 1969 and 1971, for problem banks, this ratio declined from 14.8 to 11.9 percent. On the other hand, the non-problem banks maintained between 17 and 18 percent of their assets in Treasuries.

Loan Characteristics

The investigation found that the average problem bank held between 5 and 9 percent more of its assets in loans than did the control banks. Secondly, problem banks held between 5 and 7 percent more in commercial and industrial loans (as a percentage of total loans) than did the non-problem banks. Thirdly, the ratio of interest and fees on loans to operating income was significantly higher for problem banks. For the three-year period, the average problem bank derived between 65 and 69 percent of its total operating income from loans, while the ratio for the average non-problem bank was between 58 and 59 percent. These three ratios are measures of risk in a bank's assets. As an asset, loans are more risky than the typical investment, and commercial and industrial loans generally are more risky than, say, consumer loans. Moreover, significantly higher loan ratios may indicate a lower degree of managerial ability because of the apparent willingness to accept greater potential variability in income because of the greater risk.

Efficiency

The ratio of operating expenses to operating income was used as a measure of efficiency and found to be significantly higher for problem banks. Of course, a higher ratio reflects adversely upon managerial ability to control costs and generate income. In 1971, operating expenses were 90.2 percent for the average problem bank and 81.7 percent for the average non-problem bank.

Rates of Return

Finally, the ratios of net income to assets and net income to capital were found to be significantly lower for problem banks than for non-problem banks. In 1971, the average problem bank earned only 0.5 percent on assets and 6.2 percent on capital, while the non-problem banks earned 0.9 percent on assets and 10.8 percent on capital. Again, higher earnings ratios reflect favorably on managerial ability.

In summary, Sinkey and Walker established that the average problem bank has serious shortcomings when compared with a similar non-problem bank in terms of certain traditional bank ratios. The chief value of the list of ratios in Table 7-1 is that they provide investors, corporate cash managers, bank management, and bank regulatory authorities with a convenient list of "caution signals" of possible future deterioration of a bank's financial condition.

THE N.Y. FED EARLY WARNING FUNCTION

For some years, economists at the N.Y. Federal Reserve Bank have had under study statistical techniques to warn of deteriorating bank financial condition. The goal of the research was to develop an "early warning function" which was the "smallest set of variables that could be used to detect early signs of financial deterioration."[4]

Moreover, the researchers sought to find variables for the early warning function that could be calculated from regularly reported financial data. In 1977, Korobow, Stuhr, and Martin reported a set of variables that was effective in detecting deteriorating financial condition in both regional groupings of banks and selected nationwide size classes.[5]   The authors began with the premise that, aside from outright criminal activity, there are four primary causes of bank weakness: (1) poor management, (2) erosion of earnings and capital, (3) poor internal control of expenses, and (4) unanticipated loan or investment losses.   Given these causes, the question posed by the researchers was: What financial variables in the statement of condition, the income statement, and other reported schedules indicate that one or more of these causes of financial vulnerability is present in a bank.

Of the many sets of variables analyzed, the five shown in Table 7-2 were more efficient than any other combination in detecting financial deterioration.   A decline in ratios (1), (3), (4), and (5) is indicative of vulnerability, while an increase in ratio (2) is indicative of resistance to deteriorating financial condition.   It is important to note that ratios (1), (3), and (5), in identical or almost identical form, were found to be significant by Sinkey and Walker in their study of the differences between problem and nonproblem banks.

CONCLUDING OBSERVATIONS

The two studies cited in this chapter are invaluable to everyone interested in detecting changes in bank financial condition.   It is interesting to learn that the ratios found to be significant are not "new" ratios.   Most are either identical or closely related to ratios studied in earlier chapters.   All studies show that the vast majority of

---

[4]Leon Korobow, David P. Stuhr, and Daniel Martin, "A Probabilistic Approach to Early Warning of Changes in Bank Financial Condition," Federal Reserve Bank of New York, *Monthly Review*, July, 1976, pp. 187–194.

[5]Leon Korobow, David P. Stuhr, and Daniel Martin, "A Nationwide Test of Early Warning Research in Banking," Federal Reserve Bank of New York, *Quarterly Review* (Autumn 1977), pp. 37–52.

Table 7-2. Five Early Warning Signals of Changes in Bank Financial Condition

Variable	Sign[a]
(1) $\dfrac{\text{Loans and Leases}}{\text{Total Sources of Funds}}$	–

Numerator: Loans, total domestic and foreign
+ direct lease financing

Denominator: Total domestic and foreign deposits—
cash items in process of collection + federal funds
purchased + other liabilities for borrowed money

(2) $\dfrac{\text{Equity Capital}}{\text{Adjusted Risk Assets}}$	+

Numerator: Total equity capital + loan valuation reserves +
deferred taxes of Internal Revenue Service bad debt reserve
+ minority interest in consolidated subsidiaries

Denominator: Total assets + loan valuation reserves – total
cash and due from banks (domestic offices only) – United
States Treasury securities – United States Government agency
securities – trading account securities – federal funds sold

(3) $\dfrac{\text{Operating Expenses}}{\text{Operating Revenues}}$	–

Numerator: Total operating expenses

Denominator: Total operating revenues

(4) $\dfrac{\text{Gross Charge-offs}}{\text{Net Income + Provision for Loan Losses}}$	–

Numerator: Loan losses charged to reserves

Denominator: Net operating income + provision
for loan losses

(5) $\dfrac{\text{Commercial and Industrial Loans}}{\text{Total Loans}}$	–

Numerator: Commercial and industrial loans booked
at domestic offices.

Denominator: Total gross loans booked at domestic offices

Source: Leon Korobow, David P. Stuhr, and Daniel Martin, "A Nationwide Test of Early Warning Research in Banking," Federal Reserve Bank of New York, *Quarterly Review,* (Autumn 1977), p. 41.

[a] A minus sign means an increase in the variable is indicative of vulnerability; a plus sign is indicative of resistance.

the problems of problem banks are the result of management's failure to manage properly.   It seems evident that increased familiarity and respect by management for such basic concepts as capital adequacy, liquidity, profitability, and risk aversion would go a long way to prevent a bank from becoming a problem bank.

Index